Quick and Easy Way to Learn Bengali

P. GOSWAMI

G T BOOK
AGENCY

ISBN: 81-87838-13-2

4th Published in Qualis Books 2024
Quick & Easy Way to Learn Bengali

Cover design by: **Dheeraj**

Published by
Qualis Books
140, Medha Apartment
Mayur Vihar, Ext. Phase 1,
New Delhi - 110091
E-mail : qualisbooks@yahoo.co.in

Printed in India at
D.K. Fine Art Press (P) Ltd.
Delhi - 110052

Dedicated to

Shri Samar Chakrabarty

Also Available

Quick and Easy Way to Learn	**Hindi**	**195/-**
Quick and Easy Way to Learn	**Urdu**	**195/-**
Quick and Easy Way to Learn	**Arabic**	**195/-**
Quick and Easy Way to Learn	**French**	**195/-**
Quick and Easy Way to Learn	**Japanese**	**195/-**
Quick and Easy Way to Learn	**German**	**195/-**
Quick and Easy Way to Learn	**Spanish**	**195/-**
Quick and Easy Way to Learn	**Chinese**	**195/-**
Quick and Easy Way to Learn	**Italian**	**195/-**
Quick and Easy Way to Learn	**Russian**	**195/-**

Quick and Easy Way to Learn Bengali

This book is intended for any reader who wishes to learn Bengali language and culture in 'Quick and Easy way' just for personal interest as a student, or is about to travel to this beautiful country.

As a result the grammar and the vocabulary have been confined to what might be relevant to such a reader so that self-learning process does not become a 'put-off' on coming across too much of grammar rules.

In order to facilitate the pronunciation, each word or sentence in Bengali is followed by its possible equivalent pronunciation in English.

Wish you a good luck.

E-mail: qualisbooks@yahoo.co.in

Contents

Chapter 1

Vowel - স্বরবর্ণ (Swar barna)

Letter	Pronounced as	Symbol
অ	a/all in call, hall, paul	au
আ	aa/u in palm, run	aa
ই	i in pin, tin	i/e
ঈ	ee in bee, keep	ee
উ	u in put	u
ঊ	oo in pool	oo
ঋ	ree in river, tree	ree
এ	e in pen/desk	a
ঐ	oi in join, poison	oi
ও	o in coat	o
ঔ	ou in voucher	ou

Consonant - ব্যঞ্জনবর্ণ (Byanjan barna)

Letter	Pronounced as	Symbol
ক	k/c collar, column, talk	ka
খ	kh in Ladakh	kha
গ	g in gone	ga
ঘ	gh in ghar	gha
ঙ	n in long	uan
চ	ch in bench, chalk	cha
ছ	chh in kachha	chha
জ	j/z in carzon	ja
ঝ	jh in jhum	jha
ঞ	ng in	eon
ট	t in tom, talk, ton	to
ঠ	th	tha
ড	d in don, cloud	da

ঢ	dh in dhaka	dha
ণ	n in	na
ত	t in Rajput	ta
থ	th in Rajasthan	tha
দ	d in donkey	da
ধ	dh in dharam	dha
ন	n in norm	na
প	p in palk	pau
ফ	ph/gh/f in fall, rough	ph
ব	b in ball	ba
ভ	bh/v in	bha
ম	m in monk, mortal	m
য	j in	jaw
র	r in card	raw
ল	L in long	law

শ	sh in dish	shaw
ষ	sh in push	sh
স	s in salt	s
হ	h in hall, hawk	ha
ড়	r in bhar	ra
ঢ়	rh in Asarh	rha
য়	ya in young, joy	ya
ৎ	t in Vietnam	ta
ং	n/ng in Sri Lanka, Bangladesh	n
ঃ	kh/h in	kh
ঁ	n in chand	n

Letter combinations (Akshar matra)

consonant+ Vowel	**Words**	**Pronunced as**	**Meaning**
ক+আ=কা	কাঠ	kath	wood
খ+আ=খা	খাল	khal	canal
গ+ও=গো	গোল	gol	round
ঘ+ঋ=ঘৃ	ঘৃণা	ghrina	hate
চ+ই=চি	চিতা	chita	panther
জ+আ=জা	জামা	jama	shirt
ট+ই=টি	টিকিট	ticket	ticket
ড+ই=ডি	ডিম	dim	egg
ত+এ=তে	তেল	tel	oil
থ+আ=থা	থাম	tham	piller
দ+উ=দু	দুধ	dudh	milk
ন+ঔ=নৌ	নৌকা	nauka	boat
প+এ=পে	পেরেক	perek	nail

ফ+উ=ফু	ফুল	phool	flower
ব+আ=বা	বাজ	baaj	hawk
ভ+এ=ভে	ভেড়া	bherha	sheep
ম+ঔ=মৌ	মৌমাছি	mou-maa-chhi	bee
য+অ=য	যব	job	oat
র+ও=রো	রোজ	rose	daily
ল+ও=লো	লোক	lok	man
শ+ই=শি	শিশি	shishi	bottle
হ+আ=হা	হাত	haat	hand

Simple words সরল শব্দ (Saral Sabda)

Bengali Word	Pronounced as	Meaning
জল	jal	water
পথ	path	road
বন	bon	forest
নখ	nakh	nail
কলম	kalom	pen
হজম	hajom	digest
রথ	rath	chariot
কলম	kamol	Lotus
বক	bak	crane
অধম	adham	inferior
যমজ	jamaz	twin
রতন	ratan	jewel
পতন	patan	fall

পতন	patan	fall
যখন	jakhan	when
খনন	khanon	mining
বলদ	balod	bullock
শপথ	shapath	oath
সমর	samor	battle
কলরব	kalorab	noise
নখর	nakhar	nail
খবর	khabar	news
শখ	shakh	hobby
গরম	garam	hot
পশম	pasham	wool
শরম	sharam	shame

Some Compound Letters

Joint Letters	Word	Pronunced as	Meaning
ক+য= ক্য	বাক্য	bakya	sentence
ক+র=ক্র	বিক্রয়	bikroy	sale
ল+ক=ল্ক	হাল্কা	halka	light weight
ট+ট=ট্ট	ঠাট্টা	thatta	silly talking
ম+র=ম্র	নম্র	namro	micky
ভ+র=ভ্র	অভ্র	abhro	mica
ম+ল=ম্ল	অম্ল	amlo	acidic
ত+ন=ত্ন	যত্ন	jatno	care
ন+দ=ন্দ	সন্দেহ	sandeho	suspect
ল+প=ল্প	গল্প	galpo	story
প+র=প্র	প্রহার	prohar	beating
জ+র=জ্র	বজ্র	bajro	thunder
ন+ত=ন্ত	চিন্তা	chinta	thinking

ন+ন=ন্ন	অন্ন	anno	food
ল+ম=ল্ম	গুল্ম	gulmo	shrub
ক+ল=ক্ল	ক্লান্ত	klanto	tired
গ+য=গ্য	ভাগ্য	bhagya	luck
জ+য=জ্য	রাজ্য	rajya	kingdom
ন+য=ন্য	ধান্য	dhanya	paddy
ত+য=ত্য	সত্য	satya	truth
থ+য=থ্য	মিথ্যা	mithya	false
গ+র=গ্র	উগ্র	urga	violent
ত+র=ত্র	নেত্র	netra	eye
দ+র=দ্র	ভদ্র	bhadra	gentle
ন+ত=ন্ত	শান্ত	shanta	calm
ম+প=ম্প	কম্পন	kampan	tremor

Use of Vowel aa (আ)

Bengali Word	Pronunciation	Meaning
আম	aam	mango
কান	kaan	ear
নাক	naak	nose
খাল	khal	canal
গাছ	gachh	tree
ঘাম	gham	sweat
জাল	zal	net
বাজ	baz	hawk
ডাব	dab	green coconut
ঢাক	dhak	drum
কলা	kala	banana
জবা	jaba	duranta

পাতা	pata	leaf
ছাতা	chaata	umbrella
দানা	dana	seed
খাতা	khata	copy
টাকা	taka	money
সাদা	sada	white
মামা	mama	uncle
বাবা	baba	father
গাধা	gadha	donkey
চারা	chara	sapling
মাতা	mama	mother
পাগল	pagal	mad
ছাগল	chhagal	goat
সকাল	sakal	morning

Use of Vowel e স্বরবর্ণ ইএর প্রয়োগ

Bengali Word	Pronunciation	Meaning
চিল	chil	kite (bird)
শিব	Shib	Shiva (god)
খিল	khil	latch
ছিপ	chhip	wheel-rod
ঝিল	jhil	lake
ঠিক	thik	right
ডিম	dim	egg
তিল	til	seshame
দিন	din	day
পিঠ	pith	back
শিং	sing	horn
শির	shir	head
কবি	kabi	poet

ছবি	chhabi	picture
দধি	dadhi	curd
বড়ি	bari	tablet
ঢিবি	dhibi	heap
তিমি	timi	whale
বিধি	bidhi	law
জমি	jami	land
তিসি	tisi	linseed
চিঠি	chithi	letter
পথিক	pathik	passer-by
পিতল	pital	brass
বিবর	bibar	burrow
অধিক	adhik	more
কঠিন	kathin	hard

Use of Vowel ee ঈএর প্রয়োগ

Bengali Word	Pronunciation	Meaning
কীট	kit	insect
দীন	din	poor
গীত	geet	song
ভীড়	bhir	crowd
ভীত	bhito	afraid
চীর	chir	torn cloth
জীব	jib	creature
টীকা	tika	notes
নদী	nadi	river
রথী	rathi	charioteer
পরী	pari	fairy

Use of Vowel u উএর প্রয়োগ

Bengali Word	Pronunciation	Meaning
ভুল	bhul	wrong
শুভ	shubho	good
পশু	poshu	animal
তরু	taru	tree
চুল	chul	hair
খুন	khun	murder
গুড়	gur	jaggery
দুধ	dudh	milk
মুখ	mukh	mouth
যুব	jubo	youth
খুব	khub	very

Use of Vowel oo ঊ (ূ) এর প্রয়োগ

Bengali Word	Pronunciation	Meaning
কূপ	kup	well
কূল	kul	shore
গূঢ়	gurh	concealed
চূড়া	churha	top
চূর্ণ	churno	powder
তুহিন	tuhin	ice
দূত	dut	ambassador
ধূম	dhun	smoke
নূতন	nutan	new
পূর্ব	purba	east

Use of Vowel r ঋ (ৃ) এর প্রয়োগ

Bengali Word	Pronunciation	Meaning
তৃণ	trino	grass
নৃপ	nripo	king
মৃগ	mrigo	deer
গৃহ	griho	home
বৃষ	briso	ox
মৃত	mrito	dead
তৃষা	trisa	thirst
বৃথা	britha	in vain
কৃপা	kripa	mercy
কৃষক	krisak	farmer
বৃহৎ	brihat	large
যকৃZ	jakrit	liver

Use of Vowel a এ (ে) কার এর প্রয়োগ

Bengali Word	Pronunciation	Meaning
বেল	bell	wood-apple
পেট	pet	abdomen
দেহ	deho	body
শেষ	sesh	last
তেল	tell	oil
হেম	hem	gold
পেখম	pekhom	wing
বেতন	beton	salary
অনেক	anek	many
পেরেক	perak	nail
পেঁপে	pepe	papaya
কেশ	kesh	hair

Use of Vowel oi ঐ (ৈ) কার এর প্রয়োগ

Bengali Word	Pronunciation	Meaning
শৈল	sailo	hill
বৈধ	boidho	legal
জৈব	jaibo	biological
নৈশ	noiso	night
শৈশব	soisab	childhood
দৈবাৎ	doibat	seldom
বৈকাল	boikal	afternoon
জৈন	Jain	Jain (religion)
সদৈব	sadaibo	always
অবৈধ	abaidha	illegal
মৈত্রী	maitri	friendship
গৈরিক	gairic	saffron

Use of Vowel o ও (ে া) কার এর প্রয়োগ

Bengali Word	Pronunciation	Meaning
কোন	cone	angle
চোর	chor	thief
চোখ	chokh	eye
ছোট	chhoto	small
ঢোলক	dholak	drum
তোরণ	toran	gate
পোকা	poka	insect
পোড়া	pora	burnt
বোঝা	bojha	burden
মোজা	moja	socks
মোড়ক	morak	folding
মোড়ল	moral	leader

Use of Vowel ou ঔ (ৈ া) কার এর প্রয়োগ

Bengali Word	Pronunciation	Meaning
নৌকা	nouka	boat
লৌহ	louha	iron
গৌরব	gaurav	pride
মৌমাছি	maumachhi	bee
মৌচাক	mauchak	bee-hive
বৌমা	bauma	daughter in-law
ভৌগলিক	bhougolik	geographical
সৌর	souro	solar
গৌণ	gauna	minor
পৌর	pauro	municipal
মৌন	mauno	silent
দৌলত	daulat	wealth
ভৌত	vouta	physical

Use of Vowel (anussar) ং এর প্রয়োগ

Bengali Word	Pronunciation	Meaning
হংস	hanso	drake
হংসী	hansi	duck
হিংসা	hinsa	violence
অহিংস	ahinsa	non-violence
সিংহ	sinha	lion
সিংহী	sinhi	lioness
বৃংহতি	brinhoti	trumpet
সংহার	sanhar	murder
সংহতি	sanhati	integriti
বংশ	banso	dynasty
বংশী	bonsi	flute
দংশন	donson	bite
সিংহাসন	sinhasan	throne

সংসার	sansar	family
সংবাদ	sangbad	news
লংকা	lanka	chilli
স্বয়ং	sayang	self
অংশ	ansa	part
বিংশ	binsa	twentieth
অংক	anka	maths
অংকন	ankan	drawing
ভয়ংকর	bhayankar	terrible

Chapter 2

Parts of the body

English	Bengali	Pronunciation
Abdommen	পেট	pet
Ankle	গোড়ালিরগাঁট	goralir gat
Arm	বাহু	bahu
Head	মাথা	matha
Eye	চোখ	chokh
Neck	ঘাড়	gharh
Body	শরীর	sharir
Leg	পা	pa
heel	গোড়ালী	gorali
foot	পায়ের পাতা	payer pata
finger	আঙুল	angul
belly	পেট	pet

face	মুখমণ্ডল	mukhmandal
ear	কান	kan
hair	চুল	chul
knee	হাঁটু	hatu
hand	হাত	haat
tooth	দাঁত	dant
tongue	জিভ	jiv
elbow	কনুই	konui
blood	রক্ত	rakto
flesh	মাংস	mansho
thigh	উরু	uru
rib	পাঁজরা	panjra
backbone	মেরুদণ্ড	meru danda
waist	কোমর	komor
jaw	চোয়াল	chowal

skin	চামড়া	chamra
nose	নাক	naak
mouth	মুখ	mukh
chest	বুক	book
cheek	গাল	gull
Lap	কোল	coal
finger	আঙুল	angul (hand)
toe	আঙুল	angul (leg)
brow	ভ্রূ	bhru
bone	হাড়	harh
gum	মাড়ি	marhi
nostril	নাকের ছিদ্র	nake-er-chhidro
eye-lid	চোখের পাতা	chokh-er-pata
tear	চোখের জল	chokh-er-jal
shoulder	কাঁধ	kandh

wrist	কব্জি	kabji
heart	হৃদয়	hriday
vein	শিরা	sira
stomach	পাকস্থলী	pak-sthali
brain	মস্তিষ্ক	mastiska
forehead	কপাল	kapal
lip	ঠোঁট	thot
palm	তালু	talu
spine	মেরুদণ্ড	meru-danda

Chapter 3

Animals জীবজন্তু

English	Bengali	Pronunciation
ass	গাধা	buno gadha
bull	ষাঁড়	shanrh
bullock	বলদ	balad
buffalo	মোষ	moss
cat	বিড়াল	biral
calf	বাছুর	bachhur
chameleon	গিরগিটি	girgiti
camel	উট	oot
cow	গোরু	goru
deer	হরিণ	harin
dog	কুকুর	kukur
donkey	গাধা	gadha

elephant	হাতি	hati
fox	খেঁকশিয়াল	khek-shiyal
goat	ছাগল	chhagal
hare	খরগোশ	khargosh
horse	ঘোড়া	ghora
jackal	শিয়াল	shiyal
leopard	চিতা বাঘ	chita-bagh
lion	সিংহ	singha
mare	ঘুড়ি	ghori
mongoose	বেজি	beji
monkey	বাঁদর	bandor
mouse	ইঁদুর	indur
mule	খচ্চর	khachchar
pig	শুওর	shuor
python	অজগর	ajogar
ram	ভেড়া	bherha

rhinoceras	গণ্ডার	gandar
sheep	ভেড়া, ভেড়ি	bherha (m) bherhi (f)
snake	সাপ	saap
squirrel	কাঠ বিড়াল	kath-biral
tiger	বাঘ	bagh
wolf	নেকড়ে	nekre
crab	কাঁকড়া	kankrha
crocodile	কুমির	kumir
fish	মাছ	machh
ltortise	কচ্ছপ	kachchhap
bear	ভালুক	bhaluk
frog	ব্যাঙ	bang
porcupine	সজারু	sazaru
animal	জীবজন্তু	zib-zantu
beast	পশু	Poshu

Chapter 4

Birds পাখী (Pakhi)

English	Bengali	Pronunciation
bat	বাদুড়	badurh
cock	মোরগ	morog
crane	বক	bok
crow	কাক	kaak
cuckoo	কোকিল	kokil
dove	ঘুঘু	ghu-ghu
duck	হংসী	hanshi
hen	মুরগী	murgi
kite	চিল	chil
nightingale	তোতা	tota
owl	পেঁচা	pencha
parrot	কাকাতুয়া/টিয়া	kakatua/tia

partridge	তিতির	titir
peacock	ময়ূর	mayur
pigeon	পায়রা	payra
sparrow	চড়াই	charai
swan	রাজহাঁস	rajhans
vulture	শকুন	shakun
hawk	বাজ	baaj
shallow	চাতক	chatak
kingfisher	মাছরাঙা	machh-ranga
wood pecker	কাঠঠোকরা	kath-thokra
ostrich	উটপাখি	oot-pakhi
house-bat	চামচিকে	cham-chikay
robin	বুলবুলি	bul-buli
weaverbird	বাবুই	babui
tailor bird	টুনটুনি	tun-tuni

Chapter 5

Insects and Crawlers পোকামাকড় (Poka-Makarh)

English	Bengali	Pronunciation
ant	পিঁপড়ে	piprhe
bee	মৌমাছি	maumachhi
bug	ছারপোকা	chhar-pocka
butter-fly	প্রজাপতি	proja-pati
fly	মাছি	machhi
frog	ব্যাঙ	bang
glow-worm	জোনাকি	jonaki
lizard	টিক্‌টিকি	tik tiki
locust	পঙ্গপাল	pongo-pal
mosquito	মশা	mosha
scorpion	কাঁকড়া বিছে	kankra-bichhe

spider	মাকড়সা	makarsha
snail	শামুক	shamuk
wasp	বোলতা	bolta
tortoise	কচ্ছপ	kachchhop
earth-worm	কেঁচো	kecho
leech	জোঁক	jonk
centipede	বিছে	bichhe
chameleon	গিরগিটি	girgiti
iguana	গোসাপ	go-sap
snake	সাপ	sap
cobra	গোখরো সাপ	gokhro-sap
crocodile	কুমির	kumir
germ	জীবাণু	jibanu
insect	পোকামাকড়	poka-makarh

Chapter 6

Plants গাছপালা

English	Bengali	Pronunciation
tree	গাছ	gachh
branch	ডাল	dal
seed	বীজ	beej
plant	চারা গাছ	chara gaachh
trunk	গুঁড়ি	guri
leaf	পাতা	pata
creeper	লতা	lata
root	শিকড়	shikarh
stem	ডাঁটা	danta
jute	পাট	paat
bamboo	বাঁশ	bansh
thorn	কাঁটা	kanta

mango tree	আম গাছ	aam gaachh
beetle nut tree	সুপারী গাছ	supari gaachh
pine tree	দেবদারু	deb daru
date palm tree	খেজুর গাছ	khejur gaachh
banyan tree	বট গাছ	bot gaachh
teak tree	সেগুন গাছ	segun gaachh
silk cotton tree	শিমুল গাছ	shimul gaachh
bark	ছাল	chhal
parasite	পরগাছা	por-gaachha
flowers	ফুল	phool

Chapter 7

Flowers ফুল phool

English	Bengali	Pronunciation
rose	গোলাপ	golap
chaina rose	জবা	joba
tulip	মল্লিকা	mallika
night green	রজনীগন্ধা	rajani gandha
lotus	পদ্ম	padma
sun flower	সূর্যমুখী	surya mukhi
jasmine	জুঁই	jui
stramoni	ধুতরা	dhutra
screw pine	কেতকী	ketaki
china box	কামিনী	kamini
marigold	গাঁদা	gada
water-lily	শালুক	shaluk

passion flower	ঝুমকা	jhumka
jasmine	শেফালী	shefali
gardenia	গন্ধরাজ	gandha raaj
champak	চাঁপা	champa
chameli	চামেলী	chameli
foal foot	টগর	tagor
silk dog rose	কাঠ গোলাপ	kaath golap
oleander	করবী	karabi
bastered teak	পলাশ	palash
bud	ফুলের কুঁড়ি	phool-er-kuri
garland	মালা	mala
petal	পাপড়ি	papri

Chapter 8

Fruits ফল fall

English	Bengali	Pronunciation
apple	আপেল	apel
pine apple	আনারস	anaras
wood apple	বেল	bell
pear	নাশপাতি	naspati
palm	তাল	taal
plum	কুল	kul
papaya	পেঁপে	pepe
pomgranate	বেদানা	bedana
rose-berry	গোলাপজাম	golap jam
lemon	লেবু	lebu
grapes	আঙুর	angur
green coconut	ডাব	dab
coconut	নারকেল	narkel

almond	বাদাম	badam
groundnut	চিনা বাদাম	china badam
mango	আম	aam
melon	ফুটি	futi
water melon	তরমুজ	tarmuz
cucumber	শশা	shosha
fig	ডুমুর	dumur
star apple	জামরুল	jamrul
litchi	লিচু	lichhu
guava	পেয়ারা	peyara
date	খেজুর	khejur
orange	কমলা লেবু	kamla lebu
banana	কলা	kola
jack fruit	কাঁঠাল	kanthal
black berry	কালোজাম	kalo-jam
shad dock	বাতাবি লেবু	batabi lebu

Chapter 9

House & Household articles
ঘর ও আসবাবপত্র Ghar o Asbab-patro

English	Bengali	Pronunciation
House	বাড়ি	bari
Apartment	বাসা	basa
Room	ঘর	ghar
Stair	সিঁড়ি	sirhi
Roof	ছাদ	chhad
Chair	চেয়ার	chair
Basket	ঝুড়ি	jhuri
soap	সাবান	saban
Kitchen	রান্নাঘর	ranna ghar
towel	গামছা	gamchha
mat	মাদুর	madur

bed	বিছানা	bichhana
bed-sheet	বিছানাচাদর	bichhana-chadar
bowl	বাটি	bati
box	বাক্স	bakso
brick	ইঁট	it
broom	ঝাঁটা	jhata
bucket	বালতি	balti
candle	মোমবাতি	mom-bati
cigarette	সিগারেট	cigarette
cloths-rack	আলনা	alna
corridor	বারান্দা	baranda
cottage	কুটির	kutir
court-yard	উঠান	uthan
cup	পেয়ালা	peyala
curtain	পর্দা	parda

door	দরজা	darja
fan	পাখা	pakha
ashtray	ছাইদানী	saidani
oven	তন্দুর	tandoor
plate	থালা	thala
quilt	বালিশ	balish
sack	বস্তা	bosta
spoon	চামচ	chamach
tea-cup	চায়ের পেয়ালা	cha-er-peyala
umbrella	ছাতা	chhata
wall	দেওয়াল	dewall
window	জানালা	janala

Chapter 10

Toiletries প্রসাধনী Prosadhani

English	Bengali	Pronunciation
brush	ব্রাশ	brush
dandruff	খুশকী	khuski
shampoo	শ্যাম্পু	shampoo
mouthwash	দাঁতের মাজন	dat-er-majon
perfume	সুগন্ধী	sugandhi
razor	ক্ষুর	khur
scissors	কাঁচি	kanchi
soap	সাবান	saban
tooth brush	দাঁতন	daton
towel	তোয়ালে	towale
under-garments	অর্ন্তবাস	antorbus

Where is the soap ?	সাবান কোথায়?	Saban kothai?
Give me the towel	আমাকে টাওয়েলটা দিন	Amakey towel-ta din
I don't wear undergarment	আমি অন্তর্বাস পরি না	Ami antarbas pori na
Keep Bucket &	বাথরুমে বালতি	Bathroom-a
Mug in the Washroom	ও রেখে দাও	balti o mog rakhe dao
Before to bed brush	রোজ শুতে যাবার	roj sute jabar
your teeth regularly	আগে দাঁত মাজবে	age danth majbe
Wash your hand	খাবার আগে হাত	khabar age hath
while you take food	ধোবে	dhobe
Cover food after	খাবার নিয়ে ঢাকনা	khabar niye
taking some from it. bondho	বন্ধ করবে	dhakna korbe

Chapter 11

Clothing পোশাক Poshak

English	Bengali	Pronunciation
bathing soap	গায়ে মাখা সাবান	gaye makha- saban
belt	বেল্ট	belt
blanket	কম্বল	kambal
boots	বুট জুতা	boot juto
shoes	জুতা	juto
button	বোতাম	botam
cap	টুপি	tupi
cloth	কাপড়	kapor
hat	সাহেবী টুপি	sahebi-tupi
leather	চামড়া	chamra
napkin	গামছা	gamchha
shirt	জামা	jama

thread	সুতো	suto
veil	ঘোমটা	ghomta
turban	পাগড়	pagri
this	ইহা, এই	Eha, ei
that	উহা, ঐ	uha, oi
these	ইহারা, এগুলো	Ehara, egulo
those	উহারা, ঐগুলো	uhara, oigulo
If	এটা	eta

I want to help you
আমি আপনাকে সাহায্য করতে চাই
Ami apnake sahajyo korte chai

Do you help me ?
আপনি আমাকে সাহায্য করবেন ?
Apni amakay sahajyo korben ?

What are you doing now ?
আপনি এখন কী করছেন ?
Apni ekhon ki korchhen ?

Pl. give me blanket
দয়া করে আমাকে কম্বল দাও
Daya kore Amakey kambol dao.

What is the cost of blanket ?
কম্বলের দাম কত ?
Kambol er dam koto ?

I like Red Colour blanket
লাল কম্বল আমার পছন্দ
Lal Kambol amar pachhando

Pl. give some discount
দামে ছাড় দিন
Dam e chhar din

Chapter 12

Money & Currency exchange

মুদ্রা বিনিময় mudra binimoy

English	Bengali	Pronunciation
currency	টাকা পয়সা	taka-poisa
currency-note	টাকা	taka
doller-rate	ডলারের দর	dollar er dor
foreign exchange	বিদেশী মুদ্রা বিনিময়	bideshi-mudra binimoy
exchange rate	বিনিময় দর	binimoy-dar
traveller's cheque	টুরিষ্ট চেক	tourist cheque
hallow !	শুনুন	shunun !
where can I change	কোথায় টাকা ভাঙায়	kothay taka
some money ?	বলতে পারেন ?	bhangay bolte paren ?

what is the exchange rate.	বিনিময় দর কত ?	binimoy dar kato ?
I am out of cash.	আমার কাছে টাকা পয়সা নেই।	Amar kachhe taka-poisa nei.
I would like to change money.	আমি টাকা ভাঙাতে চাই।	Ami taka bhangatey chai.
You may keep the change.	খুচরোটা আপনি রাখুন।	Khuchro ta apni rakhun.
Where is the nearest ATM ?	কাছে পিঠে কোথায় ATM বলতে পারেন ?	Kachhe-pithe ATM kothai bolte paren ?
I would like to change	আমি হাজার doller	Ami hazar
1000 doller into taka	এর বিনিময়ে টাকা নিতে চাই।	dollar er binimoy-e taka nite chai

Chapter 13

Time সময় Samay

English	Bengali	Pronunciation
Afternoon	বিকেল	bikel
An hour	এক ঘন্টা	ek-ghanta
Anniversary	বার্ষিকী	barshiki
Century	শতাব্দ	satabdo
Dawn	ভোর	bhor
Day	দিন	din
Day-to-day	রোজকার	rojkar
Decade	দশক	dasak
Evening	সন্ধ্যা	sandhya
Fortnight	পক্ষকাল	Paksho-kal
Hour	ঘন্টা	ghanta
Late	দেরী	deri

Leap year	অধিবর্ষ	adhi-varsh
Mid-day	মধ্যাহ্ন/দুপুর	dupur
Mid-night	মাঝরাত	majh-rat
Minute	মিনিট	minit
Morning	সকাল	sakal
New year	নববর্ষ	naba-varsha
Period	আমল	amal
Second	সেকেণ্ড	sekend
Some times	কখনও	kakhano
Time	সময়	Samai
This year	এ বছর	ei-bachhar
Today	আজ	aaj
This month	এ মাস	ei-mas
Now	এখন	e-khon

Past

English	Bengali	Pronunciation
Day before yesterday	গত পরশু	goto parshu
last month	গত মাসে	goto mas-e
last night	গত রাতে	goto rat-e
last week	গত সপ্তাহে	goto saptahe
last year	গত বছর	goto bachhar
two days ago	দু দিন আগে	du-din-agey
yesterday	গত কাল	goto kal

Future

English	Bengali	Pronunciation
day after tomorrow	আগামী কাল	agami kaal
in an hour	এক ঘন্টায়	ek ghantay
in five minutes	পাঁচ মিনিটে	paach-minit-e
in two days	দুদিনে	du-din-e
next month	পরের মাসে	agami mas-e

next week	পরের সপ্তাহে	parer saptai
next year	পরের বছর	parer bachhar
tomorrow	আগামী কাল	agami-kaal
What is the time ?	সময় কত ?	samay koto ?
It's 1 o'clock	এখন একটা বাজে	ekhon ekta baje
it's 2 o'clock	এখন দু'টো বাজে	ekhon duto baje
at 10 am	সকাল দশটায়	sakal dostai
it's late	দেরী হল	deri halo
Be quick	তাড়াতাড়ি কর	taratari karo
Don't waste time	সময় নষ্ট কোরো না	samay nasto karo na
Let us go	চলো যাই	cholo jai
Catch the train	ট্রেনটা ধরো	train ta dharo

Chapter 14

Week সময় Saptah

English	Bengali	Pronunciation
Monday	সোমবার	sombar
Tuesday	মঙ্গলবার	mongalbar
Wednesday	বুধবার	budhbar
Thursday	বৃহস্পতিবার	brihaspati-bar
Friday	শুক্রবার	shukrabar
Saturday	শনিবার	shanibar
Sunday	রবিবার	rabibar
Today is Sunday	আজ রবিবার	aaj rabibar
Tomorrow is Monday	কাল সোমবার	kaal sombar
Sunday is a holiday	রবিবার ছুটির দিন	rabibar chhutir-din

Chapter 15

Month মাস Mas

English	Bengali	Pronunciation
January	জানুয়ারী	January
February	ফেব্রুয়ারী	February
March	মার্চ	March
April	এপ্রিল	April
May	মে	May
June	জুন	June
July	জুলাই	July
August	আগষ্ট	August
September	সেপ্টেম্বর	September
October	অক্টোবর	October
November	নভেম্বর	November
December	ডিসেম্বর	December
January is the first	জানুয়ারী বছরের	January bachhorer
month of the year	প্রথম মাস	pratham mass

Chapter 16

Date তারিখ Tarikh

English

1. What is the date today ?
2. Today is the 23rd March.
3. On the third of this month
4. Untill 6th may

Bengali

1. আজ কত তারিখ ?
2. আজ ২৩শে মার্চ
3. এই মাসের তিন তারিখে
4. ছয়ই মে পর্যন্ত

Pronunciation

1. Aaj kato tarikh ?
2. Aaj teish-e March
3. Ei mass-er tin tarikh-e
4. Chhai-e May porjanto.

Chapter 17

Hobbies শখ Sakh

English	Bengali	Pronunciation
Cooking	রান্না	ranna
Dancing	নাচ	naach
Gardening	বাগান চর্চা	bagan charcha
Hiking	পাহাড়ে চড়া	pahar-e chara
Reading	পড়াশুনা	para-shuna
Shopping	কেনাকাটা	kena-kata
Socialising	সামাজিকতা	samajikata
Sports	খেলাধূলা	khela-dhula
Travelling	দেশ ভ্রমণ	desh-bhraman
Do you like travelling ?	তুমি কি দেশভ্রমণ পছন্দ কর ?	Tumi ki desh bhromon posando karo ?

Do you like singing ?	তুমি গান পছন্দ কর ?	Tumi gan pasando koro ?
Do you like listening to music	তুমি গান শুনতে ভালোবাসো ?	Tumi gan sunte bhalo-baso ?
Do you like watching movies ?	তুমি সিনেমা দেখতে ভালোবাসো ?	Tumi cinema dekhte bhalo baso ?
What music do you like ?	কী রকম গান তুমি পছন্দ কর ?	Ki rakam gaan tumi pasando karo ?
I like Tagore's song	আমি রবীন্দ্র সংগীত পছন্দ করি	ami Rabindra Sangeet pasando kori
I like to watch cinema	আমি সিনেমা দেখতে চাই	ami cinema dekhte chai

Chapter 18

Relationship সম্পর্ক Sampark

English	Bengali	Pronunciation
Adopted	দত্তক	dattak
Aunt	কাকীমা	kakima
Boy-friend	ছেলেবন্ধু	chhele-bandhu
Bride	কনে	konay
Bride-groom	বর	bor
Brother	ভাই	bhai
Brother-in-law	ভায়রাভাই	bhayra-bhai
Daughter	কন্যা	kanya
Daughter-in-law	বৌমা	bauma
Elder brother	বড়দা	bor-da
Elder sister	বড়দি	bor-di

Family	পরিবার	paribar
Father	বাবা	baba
Father-in-law	শ্বশুর	shashur
Girl friend	মেয়ে বন্ধু	maye-bandhu
Grand children	নাতিনাতনি	nati-natni
Grand daughter	নাতনি	natni
Grand parents	দাদুদিদা	dadu-dida
Grand-son	নাতি	nati
Guest	অতিথি	atithi
Host	গৃহস্বামী	griha-swami
Husband	স্বামী	swami
Mother	মা	maa
Mother-in-law	শাশুড়ী	sasuri
Neighbour	পড়শী	porshi
Nephew	ভাইপো	bhai-po

Niece	ভাইঝি	bhai-jhi
Parents	মাবাবা	maa-baba
Relatives	আত্মীয়	atmiya
Sister	বোন	bon
Son	পুত্র	putra
Son-in-law	জামাই	jamai
Twin brother	যমজ ভাই	jamoj bhai
Twin sister	যমজ বোন	jamoj bon
Uncle	কাকা/চাচা	kaka/chacha
Wife	পত্নী	patni
Younger brother	ছোট ভাই	chhoto-bhai
Younger sister	ছোট বোন	chhoto-bone
Wedding	বিয়ে	biye
Widow	বিধবা	bidhwa
Widower	বিধুর	bidhur

She is my mother	সে আমার মা	se amar maa
He is my brother	সে আমার ভাই	se amar bhai
She is my sister	সে আমার বোন	se amar bone
Who are you ?	কে তুমি ?	ke tumi ?
I am Yakub	আমি ইয়াকুব	ami Yakub
I am your servant sevak	আমি আপনার সেবক	ami apnar
I want to help you	আমি আপনাকে সাহায্য করতে চাই	ami apnake sahajjyo korte chai
Give me your Luggage	আপনার লাগেজ আমাকে বইতে দিন	apnar luggage amake boite din

Chapter 19

Sports খেলাধুলা Khela-dhula

English	Bengali	Pronunciation
Athelete	এ্যাথলেট	athlet
Badminton	ব্যাডমিন্টন	bad-minton
Ball	বল	bol
Bat	ব্যাট	bat
Bull fight	ষাঁড়ের লড়াই	shar-er-lorai
Coach	প্রশিক্ষক	prosikshak
Cricket	ক্রিকেট	criket
Defeat	পরাজয়	parajoy
Foot ball	ফুটবল	fut-bol
Foul	ফাউল	foul
Game	খেলা	khela

Goal	লক্ষ্য	lakhya
Group	দল	dal
Match	খেলা	khela
Play ground	খেলার মাঠ	khelar-math
Sportsman	খেলোয়াড়	kheloar
Swimmer	সাঁতারু	sataru
Swimming	সাঁতার	satar
Team	দল	dal
Victory	জয়	joy
Winner	বিজয়ী	bijoyi
Do you like sport ?	তুমি খেলাধূলা পছন্দ কর নাকি?	Tumi khela-dhula pasand karo naki ?
Yes, very much	হ্যাঁ, খুব ভালো লাগে	ha, khub bhalo lagey
Not really	না, ততটা নয়	na, tatota noi

Would you like to go to a cricket match ?	ক্রিকেট খেলা দেখতে যেতে চাও ?	kriket khela dekhte jete chao ?
What is the score now ?	কত স্কোর হয়েছে এখন ?	kato score hoyechhe ekhon ?
It is a draw	খেলা ড্র হয়েছে ?	khela draw hoyeche
How much time	আর কত সময় বাকি ?	Ar kato somoy baki ?
What sports do you play ?	তুমি কোন খেলা করতে পারো ?	tumi kon khela korte paro ?
Who is your favourite sportsman ?	তোমার প্রিয় খেলোয়াড় কে ?	Tomar priyo khelowar ke ?

Chapter 20

Ailments পীড়াবিষয়ক Peera-bisayak

English	Bengali	Pronunciation
Accident	দুর্ঘটনা	dur-ghatana
Acidity	অ্যাসিডিটি	acidity
Allergy	এলার্জি	allergy
Ambulance	এ্যামবুলেন্স	ambulance
Anesthetic	চেতনা নাশক	chetna-nashak
Antibiotic	বীজঘ্ন	bijaghna
Inflamatory	প্রদাহ	pro-daho
Asthma	শ্বাসকষ্ট	sas-kasto
Bandage	ব্যাণ্ডেজ	bandage
Bleeding	রক্তপাত	rakto-pat
Blindness	অন্ধত্ব	and-hot-to

Blood	রক্ত	rakto
Blood Pressure	রক্তচাপ	rakto-chap
Burn	পোড়া	Pora
Cataract	ছানি	chhani
Chickenpox	জলবসন্ত	jal-basanta
Cholera	কলেরা	kolera
Clinic	চিকিৎসালয়	chik-it-sa-laya
Constipation	কোষ্ঠবদ্ধতা	kostho-boddhota
Contact	চুক্তি	chukti
Cough	কাশি	kasi
Cure	সারা	Sara
Diabetes	মধুমেহ	madhu-meho
Diarrhea	ডায়ারিয়া	dia-ria
Disease	রোগ	rogue
Dispensary	চিকিৎসালয়	chick-it-salay

Doctor	চিকিৎসক	chick-it-sok
Epidemic	মহামারি	mahamari
faint	মূর্চ্ছা	murchha
fever	জ্বর	jor
food-poisoning	খাদ্য বিষক্রিয়া	khaddya-biso-kriya
Glasses	কাঁচ	kanch
Gynecologist	স্ত্রী রোগ বিশেষজ্ঞ	stri-rog-bisesagya
Headache	মাথা ব্যথা	matha-betha
Heart	হৃদয়	hridoy
Heart-attack	হার্টএ্যাটাক	heart attack
Homeopathy	হোমিওপ্যাথি	homeopathy
Hospital	হাসপাতাল	hospital
Hunger	ক্ষুধা	khudha
Indigestion	অজীর্ণ	a-jir-no
Infection	সংক্রমণ	san-kra-man

Inflamation	প্রদাহ	prodaha
Jaundice	জণ্ডিস	jondish
Leoprosy	কুষ্ঠ	kustha
Leukemia	লিউকোমিয়া	lucomia
Madness	উন্মাদরোগ	un-mad-rogue
Measles	হাম	hum
Medicine	ওষুধ	osudh
Mumps	কর্ণমূল প্রদাহ	karna-mul pradaha
Pain	ব্যথা	betha
Paralysis	প্যারালাইসিস	paralisis
Pharmacy	ঔষধালয়	ousad-a-lay
Piles	অর্শ	arsho
Pregrant	গর্ভবতী	garva-bati
Pulse	নাড়ি	nari
Pus	পূঁজ	puj

Rheumatism	বাত	but
Saliva	লালা	lala
Shiver	কাঁপ	kap
Sick	পীড়িত	pirito
Side-effect	পার্শ্বপ্রতিক্রিয়া	parsva-prati-kriya
Sleeping-pill	ঘুমের বড়ি	ghum-er-bori
Sneeze	হাঁচি	hanchi
Stomach-ache	পেট ব্যথা	pet-byatha
Sun burn	রোদে ঝলসানো	rode-jhalsano
Surgery	অস্ত্রোপচার	astro-patcher
Sweat	ঘাম	gham
Swelling	ফোলা	phola
Tablet	বড়ি	bori
Thermometer	থার্মোমিটার	tharmo-meter
Treatment	চিকিৎসা	chikit-sa

Tumor	টিউমার	tumar
Urine	পেচ্ছাব	pet-sab
Vomiting	বমি	bomi
Weak	দুর্বল	durball
Wound	ক্ষত	khat
Is there a Chemist shop nearby ?	কাছে পিঠে কোন ওষুধের দোকান আছে ?	kachhe kono osudher dokan achhe ?
Where is the nearest hospital?	নিকটতম হাসপাতালটি কোথায় ?	nikat-tamo haspatal kothai ?
Where is the Casualty ?	দুর্ঘটনা কোনখানে ঘটেছে ?	durghatona konkhane ghatechhe ?
What are the visiting hours ?	দেখার সময় কখন ?	dekhar samay kokhon ?

Whare is word no 6 ?	ছ' নম্বর ওয়ার্ডটি কেন দিকে ?	chha namber-er word-te kon dikey?
I need the medicine please	আমার ওষুধের দরকার	amar osudher darkar
Please give me medicine to cure	দয়া করে রোগ সারার ওষুধ দিন	daya korey rogue sarar osudh din
I have the prescription	আমার কাছে প্রেসক্রিপসন আছে	amar kachhe prescription achhe
How many times a day ?	দিনে ক'বার ওষুধ খেতে হবে ?	diney ko-bar osudh khete hobe ?
Twice a day	দিনে দু'বার	diney du-bar
Have you taken this before ?	আগে কখনো কি ওষুধ নিয়েছেন ?	Agey kakhono ki osudh niyechen ?
It is made according	প্রেসক্রিপশন মতোই	prescription
to prescription	এটা তৈরী করা	kmotoi eta toiri kora
I feel sick	আমি অসুস্থ বোধ করছি	cami asustho bodh korchi

I suffer from rheumatick	আমি বাতের ব্যথায় ভুগছি	ami bat-er byathai bhugchi
Please get the doctor	দয়া করে ডাক্তারের কাছে চলুন	daya korey docter-er kachhe chalun
Quick! Help! Medical care	জলদি! বাঁচান! ওষুধ দিন!	zaldi! bachan! osudh din!
Can I see a female doctor ?	কোন মহিলা ডাক্তারকে দেখানো যাবে ?	kono mahila doctor-ke dakhano jabey ?
Which doctor is treating you ?	কোন ডাক্তার তোমাকে দেখছেন ?	kon daktor tomakey dekhchhen ?
I can not tolerate the heat	গরম সহ্য করতে পারছি না	gorom sojjo korte parchhi na
The doctor prescribed to take rest	ডাক্তার পুরোপুরি বিশ্রাম নিতে বলেছেন	daktar puropuri bishram nitey boleechhen

I have a tooth-ache	আমার দাঁতে ব্যথা হচ্ছে	amar dat-e bathe hochchhe
Where does it hurt you	তোমার কোথায় আঘাত লেগেছে	tomar kothai aghat lagechhe ?
I don't have an appetite	আমার ক্ষিধে নেই	amar khidey nei
How do you feel ?	কেমন বোধ করছেন ?	kemon bodh korchen ?
I fell down the stairs	সিঁড়ি থেকে আমি পড়ে গেছি ?	Siri theke ami porey gechhi
You need to be admitted to hospital	আমার হাসপাতালে ভর্তি হওয়া দরকার	Amar hospatal-e bhorti howa darkar
He needs a blood transfusion	তাকে রক্ত দিতে হবে	takey rakto ditey hobe
What is your blood group ?	তোমার ব্লাড গ্রুপ কি?	tomar blood group ki ?
Can you donate	রক্ত দান করতে পারবেন ?	rakto dan blood kortey parben ?

Please use new syringe	দয়া করে একটা একটা নতুন সিরিঞ্জ ব্যবহার করুন	daya korey ekta a notun syringe babohar karun
I think I am pragnant	মনে হচ্ছে আমি গর্ভবতী হয়ে গেছি	mone hoy ami garvobati hoye gachi
Are you using contraceptive ?	তুমি কি গর্ভ নিরোধক ব্যবহার করছ ?	tumi ki garbho nirodhak babohar karchho ?
I did not want to be pregnent	আমি গর্ভবতী হতে চাইনি।	ami garbho-boti hote chaini
Let us go to a doctor	চলো ডাক্তারের কাছে যাই	cholo doctor-er kachhe jai
She will help you	তিনি তোমাকে সাহায্য করবেন	tini tomake sahajjyo korben
Then we shall	তারপর আমরা সিদ্ধান্ত নেবো	tarpor amra siddhanto nebo

Chapter 21

Around the town
শহরবিষয়ক Sahar bisayak

English	Bengali	Pronunciation
Airport	বিমান বন্দর	Biman Bondor
Area	এলাকা	elaka
Bakery	বেকারী	bekari
Bar	বার	bar
Barber shop	নাপিতের দোকান	napiter dokan
Bazaar	বাজার	bazar
Beach	সৈকত	saikat
Beauty Parlour	বিউটি পার্লার	beauty parlour
Bicycle	বাইসাইকেল	bi-cycle
Book shop	বইএর দোকান	boi-er-dokan
Border	সীমানা	simana

Bridge	ব্রিজ	bridge
Building	বিল্ডিং	building
Bus	বাস	bus
Bucher's shop	কসাইএর দোকান	kasai-er-dokan
Cafe	কাফে	kafe
Capital City	রাজধানী	rajdhani
Carpenter	ছুতোর মিস্ত্রি	chutor mistri
Cart	গরুর গাড়ি	gorur gari
Castle	দুর্গ	durgo
Cave	গুহা	guha
Chemist shop	ওষুধের দোকান	osudher dokan
Church	গীর্জা	girja
Club	ক্লাব	club
Cinema	সিনেমা	cinema
City	শহর	sahar

Country	দেশ	desh
Cottage	ঘর	Ghar
Court (Law)	আদালত	Adalat
Crowd	জনতা	Janata
District	জিলা	Zila
Ditch	গর্ত	Garto
Factory	কারখানা	Karkhana
Farm	খামার	Khamar
Farm house	খামার বাড়ি	Khamar Bari
Fence	বেড়া	Bera
Field	মাঠ	math
Fish Market	মাছের বাজার	Macher Bazar
Flower Shop	ফুলের দোকান	Ful-er-dokan
Fort	দূর্গ	Durgo
Fountain	ঝর্ণা	Jharna

Fruit shop	ফলের দোকান	Phal-er-dokan
Furniture shop	আসবাবএর দোকান	Asbab-er-dokan
Garden	বাগান	Bagan
Gate	প্রবেশ পথ	Prabesh Path
Grave Yard	কবর খানা	Kabar-khana
Green Grocer's Shop	সব্জীর দোকান	Sabjir dokan
Guest House	অতিথি নিবাস	Atithi niwas
Harbour	পোতাশ্রয়	Pot-ashray
Hat shop	টুপির দোকান	Tupi-r-dokan
Hill	পাহাড়	Pahar
Hospital	হাসপাতাল	Haspatal
Inn	সরাইখানা	Sarai Khana
Jewellery Shop	জুয়েলারী দোকান	Jewelary dokan
Lane	গলি	Goli

Library	গ্রন্থাগার	Granthagar
Liquor Store	মদের দোকান	Mod-er-dokan
Lost & Found	হারানোপ্রাপ্তি	Harano-prapti
Market	বাজার	Bazar
Maternity home	প্রসূতি সদন	Prasuti Sadan
Ministry	মন্ত্রণালয়	Mantranalaya
Mosque	মসজিদ	Mosjid
Mountain	পর্বত	Parbat
Mountain Range	পর্বতমালা	Parbat mala
Museam	যাদুঘর	Jadughar
National Park	জাতীয় উদ্যান	Jatiyo Uddan
Night Club	নাইট ক্লাব	Night Club
Optician's Shop	চশমার দোকান	Chasmar dokan
Orphanage	অনাথাশ্রম	Anathashram
Park	উদ্যান	Uddan

Restaurant	ভোজনালয়	Bhojanalaya
River	নদী	Nadi
Road	রাস্তা	Rasta
School	বিদ্যালয়	Bidyalaya
Shop	দোকান	Dokan
Street	রাস্তা	rasta
Tailor's Shop	দরজির দোকান	Dorjir dokan
Temple	মন্দির	Mandir
Tomb	সমাধি	Samadhi
Town	শহর	Sahar
Tree	গাছ	Gachh
University	বিশ্ববিদ্যালয়	Bishwa-vidyalay
Valley	উপত্যকা	Upatyaka
Village	গ্রাম	Gram
Wall	দেওয়াল	Dewal

Burka	বোরখা	Borkha
Umbrella	ছাতা	Chata
Flower vase	ফুলদানী	Phul Dani
Marriage	শুভ বিবাহ	Shubho bibaha
I would like to confirm my ticket	আমি আমার টিকিট কনফার্ম করতে চাই	Ami amar ticket confirm korte chai
I would like to cancel my ticket	আমি আমার টিকিট ক্যানসেল করতে চাই	Ami amar ticket cancel korte chai
Are children allowed ?	শিশুদের অ্যালাউ করা হবে কি ?	Sisuder allow kora hobe ki ?
Is Lunch included ?	সাথে লাঞ্চ পাবো ?	Sathe lunch pabo ki ?
I want to see local sights	আমি লোকাল সাইট দেখতে চাই	Ami local sight dekhte chai
Where do we meet ?	আমাদের কোথায় দেখা হবে ?	Amader kothai dakha hobe ?

When do you meet ?	কখন আমরা দেখা করবো ?	Kokhan amra dekha korbo?
How long does the trip take ?	ঘুরতে কত সময় লাগবে ?	Ghurte koto samay lagbe ?
When does the tour Start ?	ট্যুর কখন শুরু হবে ?	Tour kokhan suru hobe ?
Where are the toilets ?	টয়লেট কোনদিকে বলতে পারেন ?	Toilet kon dike bolte paren ?
Give me five minutes	আমাকে পাঁচ মিনিট সময় দিন	amake panch minute samoy din
I want to go toilet	আমি টয়েলেটে যেতে চাই	ami toilet-e jete chai
can we hire a guide ?	একজন গাইড ভাড়া পাওয়া যাবে ?	Ekjon guide bhara pawa jabe ?
When do we start off ?	আমাদের যাত্রা কখন শুরু হবে ?	Amader jatra kakhon suru hobe ?
When do we get back ?	আমরা কখন ফিরবো ?	Amra kakhon firbo ?

Chapter 22

Directions দিক (Dik)

English	Bengali	Pronunciation
Behind	পেছনে	Pechhane
East	পূব দিকে	Pub dike
Far away	অনেক দূরে	Anek dur
Here	এখানে	Ekhane
In front of	সামনে	Samne
Left	বামে	Balme
Near	কাছে	Kachhe
North	উত্তর	Uttar
North-East	উত্তরপূব	Uttar-Pub
North-West	উত্তর পশ্চিম	Uttar-Paschim
Opposite	উল্টো দিক	Ulto-dik
Right	ডাইনে	Daine

South	দক্ষিণ	Dakshin
South-East	দক্ষিণপূব	Dakshin-Pub
South-West	দক্ষিণপশ্চিম	Dakshin Paschim
Straight ahead	সোজা সামনে	Soja-Samne
There	সেখানে	Sekhane
Turn Left	বামে যান	Bame jan
Turn Right	ডাইনে যান	Daine jan
West	পশ্চিম	Paschim
Go to the East	পূব দিকে যান	Pub dikey jan
Turn at the corner	কোনাটায় গিয়ে ঘুরে যান	Konatai giye ghurey jan
Turn at the traffic light	লালবাতিতে গিয়ে ঘুরে যান	Lal batitey giye ghurey jan

Chapter 23

On the Telephone টেলিফোনে কথাবার্তা (Telephone-e kotha-barta)

English	Bengali	Pronunciation
Hallo	হ্যালো	Halo
Is Mr. Sen there	মিঃ সেন আছেন ?	Mr. Sen achhen?
Can I speak to Mr. Sen	মিঃ সেনের সাথে কথা বলা যাবে ?	Mr. Sen-er sathe kotha bola jabe ?
Who are you speaking ?	কে বলছেন ?	Kay bolchhen ?
I am Saikat speaking	আমি সৈকত বলছি	Ami Saikat bolchi
Who do you want to speak ?	কার সাথে কথা বলতে চান ?	Kar sathe kotha bolte chan ?
Where are you calling from ?	কোথা থেকে বলছেন ?	Kotha thake bolchhen

I am calling from Diamond Harbour	আমি ডায়মণ্ড হারবার থেকে বলছি	Ami Diamond Harbour theke bolchi
You have the wrong number	আপনি ভুল নম্বরে ফোন করেছেন	Apni bhul number-e phone korechhen
Whose call is it ?	কে ফোন করেছে ?	Ke phone korechhe ?
The line is busy	লাইন ব্যস্ত রয়েছে	Line byasto royechhe
All lines are engaged	সব লাইনই ব্যস্ত	sob line-e byasto
Where is the nearest public phone ?	কাছে পাবলিক ফোন কোথায় ?	kachhe public phone kothai ?

Chapter 24

Customs কাষ্টম (Kastom)

English	Bengali	Pronunciation
Can I see your passport please?	আপনার পাসপোর্ট দেখতে পারি?	Apnar Passport dakhte pari
I have articles of my personal use	আমার নিজের কিছু জিনিসপত্র আছে	Amar nijer kichhu jinis patra achhe
Please open	দয়া করে খুলুন	Doya kore khulun
This is a Present	এটা একটা উপহার	Eta ekta upahar
That is my Suitcase	ওটা আমার সুটকেস	Ota amar suitcase
Do I have to pay duty in...	আমাকে কি ডিউটি দিতে হবে ?	Amake ki duty dite hobe ?
It is a bottle of perfume	এটা এক বোতল সুগন্ধি	Eta ek botol sugandhi

It belongs to me	এটা আমার	Eta amar
I have purchased from Kolkata	আমি এটা কোলকাতা থেকে কিনেছি	Ami eta Kolkata theke kinechhi
I would like to declare ...	আমি ঘোষণা করতে চাই ...	Ami ghosana korte chai ...
May I sit here ?	এখানে একটু বসতে পারি ?	Ekhane ektu boste pari ?
One of my	আমার একটা	Amar ekta
luggage has been lost	লাগেজ হারিয়ে গেছে।	luggage harie gechhe

Chapter 25

At the Restaurant
রেস্টুরেন্টএ (Resturent-e)

Is there a good Chinese Restaurant here ?
এখানে কোনো ভাল চাইনিজ রেস্টুরেন্ট আছে ?
Ekhane kono bhalo chinese resturent achhe ?

Which restaurant is the cheapest here ?
এখানে কোন রেস্টুরেন্টটা সবচেয়ে সস্তা ?
Ekhane kon resturent ta sob chaye sasta ?

Is there a vegetarian restaurant here ?
এখানে কি কোন ভেজিটারিয়ান রেস্টুরেন্ট আছে ?
Ekhane ki kono vegetarian restaurant achhe ?

Are you still serving food ?
আপনারা কি এখনো খাবার দিচ্ছেন ?
Apnara ki ekhono khabar dichchhen ?

What is the menu ?
মেনু তে কি আছে ?
Menu te ki achhe ?

Do you have a menu in English ?
ইংরাজীতে লেখা কোনো মেনু আছে ?
Engraji-te lekha kono menu achhe ?

Please bring a glass
দয়া করে একটা গ্লাস দিন না
Doya kore ekta glass din na

How long is the wait ?
আর কতক্ষণ অপেক্ষা করবো ?
Ar kotokhan opekkha korbo ?

Some water please
দয়া করে একটু জল দিন !
Doya kore ektu zal din

I don't eat any meat
আমি কোন মাংস খাই না
Ami kono mangso khai na

Does it take long to prepare ?
তৈরী হতে কী সময় লাগবে ?
Toiri hote ki samay lagbe ?

May I have a dance with you ?
তোমার সাথে আমাকে নাচতে দেবে ?
Tomar sathe amake nachte debe ?

I want to have a cigarette
আমি সিগারেট খেতে চাই
Ami cigarette khete chai

I don’t want it deep fried
বেশী ভাজতে হবে না
Besi bhaja hone na

My bill please
দয়া করে বিলটা দিন
Daya kore bill-ta din

Chapter 26

At the Bar
পানশালায় (Pan-salay)

Please serve me a peg whisky
আমাকে এক পেগ হুইস্কি দিন
Amake ek peg whisky din

Cheers !
চিয়ার্স
Cheers !

Do you like soda with it ?
আপনি কি সোডা নিতে চান ?
Apni ki soda nite chan ?

Excuse me !
মাফ করবেন !
Maaf korben !

We drink it straight
আমি একদমে পান করি।
Ami ek-dom-e pan kori

I am feeling drunk
আমার নেশা ধরে গেছে
Amar nesha dhorey gechhe

No ice, thanks
বরফ লাগবে না, ধন্যবাদ
Baraf lagbe na, dhanyabad

Will you have a drink ?
এক চুমুক নেবেন নাকি ?
Ak chumuk neben naki ?

The wine is extra
অনেকটা মদ রয়েছে
Khanikta mod royechhe

You can get the next one
আরো একটু নিতে পারেন
Aro ektu nite paren

Chapter 27

Pronouns সর্বনাম (Sarbo-nam)

I	আমি	Ami
We	আমরা	Amra
Our	আমাদের	Amader
Us	আমাদিগকে	Amadigake
You	তুমি, তুই, আপনি,	Tumi, Tui, Apni,
	তোমরা, তোরা, আপনারা	Tomra, Tora, Apnara
Your	তোমার, তোর, আপনার,	Tomar, Tor,
	তোমাদের, তোদের,	Apnar, Tomader,
	আপনাদের	Toder, Apnader
He/She	সে	se
Him/her	তাকে/তাহাকে	Takay/Tahakay
Them	তাহাদিগকে	Tahadigakay
Their	তাহাদের	Tahader
Who	কে / কারা	ke /kara
Whom	কাকে	kake
it	ইহা	yiha
here	এখানে	ekhaney

Chapter 28

At the Hotel হোটেলে (Hotel-e)

I would like to book a room please
আমি একটা রুম বুক করতাম
Ami ekta room book kortam

How much is it per night ?
প্রতি রাতের ভাড়া কত লাগবে ?
Prati rater bhara kato lagbe ?

Single room or double room ?
সিঙ্গাল রুম নাকি ডবল রুম ?
Single room nake double room ?

AC or non-AC
এ.সি. আছে নাকি নেই ?
AC achhe naki nei ?

Which room is assigned to me ?
আমাকে কোন রুমটা দিলেন ?
Amake kon room-ta dilen ?

I would prefer the first floor
আমি ফার্স্ট ফ্লোরে নিতে চাইছি
Ami first floor-e nite chaichhi

What is the check-out time ?
চেক্ আউট টাইম কখন ?
Check-out time kakhan ?

Can I leave my bags here ?
আমার ব্যাগগুলো এখানে রাখতে পারি কি ?
Amar bag-gulo ekhane rakhte pari ki ?

Could you come back later, please ?
আপনি কি পরে আসতে পারবেন ?
Apni ki pore aste parben ?

Please wake me at seven
দয়া করে আমাকে সাতটার সময় জাগিয়ে দেবেন
Daya kore amake sat-tar samay jagiye deven

Is there any message for me ?
আমার জন্য কি কোন খবর আছে ?
Amar jonye ki kono khabar achhe ?

There is a letter address to Golam Ali
গোলাম আলির নামে একটা চিঠি এসেছে
Golam Ali-r name ekta chithi esechhe

It came this morning
এটা আজ সকালে এসেছে
Eta aaj sakale esechhe

Do you also arrange tours ?
আপনারা ট্যুরএর ব্যবস্থা করেন নাকি ?
Apnara tour er o byabastha koren naki ?

Can you call a taxi for me ?
আমার জন্য একটা ট্যাক্সি ডেকে দিতে পারেন ?
Amar jonyo ekta taxi deke dite paren ?

I will pay at the time of check-out.
চেক আউটের সময় পেমেন্ট করবো।
Check-out

Here is your tips.
এখানে তোমার টিপ্‌স রহিল
Akhene tips rohilo.

Chapter 29

Complaints নালিশ (Nalish)

The shower doesn't work
শাওয়ারটা কাজ করছে না
Shower-ta kaj korchhe na

The door of my room no-202 doesn't close properly
রুম নং ২০২এর দরজা ঠিকমতো বন্ধ হচ্ছে না
Room no. 202 er doroja thikmato bandho hochche na

The lift is stuck at the seventh floor
লিফট সাত তলায় আটকে রয়েছে
Lift sat-tolay atkey royechhe

The fan does not work
পাখা ঘুরছে না
Pakha ghurchhe na

The toilet is not clean
টয়লেট পরিস্কার নয়।
Toilet pariskar noi.

There is a cockroach in the bathroom.
বাথরুমে একটা আরশোলা রয়েছে ।
Bathroom-e ekta arshola royechhe.

The room is too dark.
ঘরটা খুবই অন্ধকার।
Ghar-ta khub andhokar

The window does not open properly
জানালাটা ঠিক মতো খোলে না।
Janala-te thikmoto khole na

The room is too small
ঘরটা খুব ছোট.
Gharta khub chhoto

Chapter 30

Asking the way পথ জানা (Path jana)

Am I right for the airport ?
এয়ারপোর্টের রাস্তায় যাচ্ছি তো ?
Airport er rastay jachchhi to ?

Are we on the right way ?
আমরা কি ঠিক রাস্তায় চলেছি ?
Amra ki thik rastay cholechhi ?

Can you direct me to the market ?
বাজারের পথটা দেখিয়ে দেবেন ?
Bazar-er path-ta dekhiye deben ?

How far is it to the airport ?
এয়ার পোর্ট থেকে জায়গাটা কত দূরে ?
Airport theke zaigata koto durey ?

It is 10 Kilometres to the palace.
এটা প্যালেস থেকে ১০ কি.মি. দূরে
Eta palace theke dos kilometre durey ?

This road meets up with the moterway.
এই রাস্তাটা মোটর রোডে গিয়ে মিশেছে।
Ei rastata motor road-a giye mishechhe.

Where do we go from here ?
এখান থেকে আমরা কোথায় যাবো ?
Ekhan theke amra kothay jabo ?

We have a long way to go.
আমাদের অনেকটা পথ যেতে হবে।
Amader anek-ta poth jete hobe.

Chapter 31

Taxi ট্যাক্সি (Taxi)

Please take me to this address.
দয়া করে আমাকে এই ঠিকানায় নিয়ে চলুন।
Doya kore amake ei thikanai niye chalun.

Please put the meter on.
দয়া করে মিটার চালু রাখুন।
Daya kore meter chalu rakhun.

How much is the final fare ?
মোট কত ভাড়া লাগবে ?
Mot kato bhara lagbe ?

Please slow down.
দয়া করে আস্তে চালান।
Daya kore astey chalan.

Please wait here
দয়া করে এখানে অপেক্ষা করুন।
Doya kore ekhane apeksha korun.

Stop at the corner.
এই কোণে থামান।
Ei kone-e thaman.

Please help me to get the bags down.
ব্যাগ গুলো নামাতে সাহায্য করুন।
Bag gulo namate sahajjyo korun.

Stop here.
এখানে থামুন।
Ekhane thamun.

Why do you charge extra from me ?
ভাড়া বেশী নিচ্ছেন কেন ?
Bhara beshi nicchen keno ?

Chapter 32

In the Police Station থানায় (Thanay)

I would like to report a theft.
আমি চুরির রিপোর্ট লেখাতে চাই।
Ami churi-r report lekhat-e chai.

I have lost my passport / purse.
আমার পাসপোর্ট/পার্স হারিয়ে গেছে।
Amar passport / purse hariye gechhe.

I have been robbed.
আমার সবকিছু ডাকাতে নিয়ে গেছে।
Amar sob kichhu dakate niye gechhe.

I want to contact my embassy / consulate.
আমার এমব্যাসী/কনস্যুলেটের সাথে যোগাযোগ করতে চাই।
Amar embassy / consulate-er sahe jogajog korte chai.

I need a lawyer to speaks english.
ইংরাজী জানা একজন উকিল চাই।
Engraji jana akjon ukil ami chai.

It is not my fault.
আমার কোন দোষ নেই।
Amar kono dosh nei

Can I pay an on-the-spot fine ?
আমি অনদাস্পট জরিমানা দিতে পারবো কি ?
Ami on-the-spot jarimana dite parbo ki ?

I would like to report a theft.
আমি চুরির রিপোর্ট লেখাতে চাই।
Ami churi-r report lekhate chai.

I apologise
আমি ক্ষমা চাইছি।
Ami khama chai-chi.

Chapter 33

In the Bank ব্যাঙ্কে (Bank-e)

I would like to cash a cheque.
আমি একটা চেক ভাঙিয়ে ক্যাশ করতে চাই।
Ami ekta chek bhangiye cash korte chai.

I would like to change money.
আমি টাকায় বদলাতে চাই।
Ami takai bodlate chai.

What time does the bank open ?
কোন সময় ব্যাঙ্কটা খোলে ?
Kon samay bank-ta kholey ?

Can I arrange a transfer ?
আমি ট্রান্সফারএর ব্যবস্থা করতে পারবো ?
Ami transfer-er byabostha korte parbo ?

I have forgotten my pin no.
আমি আমার পিন নম্বর ভুলে গেছি।
Ami amar pin no bhule gechhi.

What is the exchange rate ?
মুদ্রা বিনিময় দর কত চলছে ?
Mudra binimoy dar koto chalchhe ?

Can I see your passport please.
আপনার পাসপোর্টটা দেখতে পারি।
Apnar passport-ta ki dekhte pari.

I have 500 dollar with me
আমার কাছে পাঁচশ ডলার আছে।
Amar kachhe panch-sho dollar achhe.

You gave me one extra dollar.
আপনি আমাকে একটা বেশী ডলার দিয়েছেন।
Aponi amake akta besi dollar diyechen.

I want to keep ornaments in the locker.
আমি লকারে গহণাগুলি রাখতে চাই।
Ami Locker-e gohonaguli rakhte chai.

Chapter 34

At the Border বর্ডারে (Border-e)

Your passport please.
আপনার পাসপোর্টটা দেখাবেন ?
Apnar passport-ta dekhaben ?

Are you travelling in a group ?
আপনি কি দল বেঁধে ঘুরছেন ?
Apni ki dol bedhe ghurchhen ?

Are you travelling on your own ?
আপনারা নিজেদের জিম্মায় ঘুরছেন নাকি ?
Apnara nijeder jimmai ghurchhen naki ?

Your paper please.
আপনার কাগজপত্র দয়া করে দেখান।
Apnar Kagaj-patro daya kore dekhan.

What is the purpose of visit ?
কী উদ্দেশ্যে বেড়াতে এসেছেন ?
Ki uddeshye berate eashechhen ?

I am here on holiday ?
আমি এখানে ছুটি কাটাতে এসেছি।
Ami ekhane chhuti korate eschechhi.

I am here for 2 weeks.
আমি এখানে দুসপ্তাহর জন্য এসেছি।
Ami ekhane du-saptar jonno esechhi.

I want to visit Bangladesh.
আমি বাংলাদেশে ঘুরতে চাই।
Ami Bangladesh ghurte chai.

What thing I have to carry to Sundarban ?
সুন্দরবনে যেতে হলে কি কি নিয়ে যেতে হবে ?
Sundarbone jate hole ki ki niye jate hobe ?

Chapter 35

Socialising সামাজিকতা (Samajikata)

Are you free tomorrow ?
আগামীকাল আপনি কি ফ্রি আছেন ?
Agami kal apni ki free achhen ?

What are you doing this evening ?
আজ সন্ধ্যায় কি করছেন ?
Aj Sandhay ki korchhen ?

Would you like to go for a drink ?
মদ্য পান করতে যাবেন নাকি ?
Madira pan korte jaben naki ?

Can you come to dinner ?
ডিনার খেতে আসতে পারবেন?
Dinner khete aste parben ?

Are you ready ?
আপনি কি তৈরী আছেন ?
Apni ki toiri achhen ?

Will you join me in a drink ?

মদ খেতে আপনারা আমাকে দলে নেবেন?

Mod khete apnara amake dale neben ?

Would you like to go for a walk ?

হাঁটতে যেতে চান নাকি?

Hat-te jete chan naki ?

Let us take our dinner.

চলুন ডিনার খাওয়া যাক।

Chalun dinner khaoa jak.

Varieties of flowers in the park.

পার্কে বিভিন্ন রকমের ফুল পাওয়া যায়।

Park-e bivinno rokomer phool paoa jai.

Chapter 36

Small talks টুকটাক কথা (Tuk-tak kotha)

Good morning sir / madam.
গুড মর্নিং স্যর/ম্যাডাম।
Good morning sir / madam.

How are you ?
কেমন আছেন ?
Kemon achhen ?

What is your name ?
আপনার নাম ?
Apnar naam ?

My name is ....
আমার নাম ....
Amar naam ....

Where do you come from ?
আপনি কোথা থেকে আসছেন ?
Apni kotha theke aschhen ?

I am from London.
আমি লণ্ডন থেকে আসছি।
Ami London theke aschhi.

Where are you going ?
কোথায় যাচ্ছেন ?
Kothai jachchhen ?

Do you speak English ?
ইংরেজি বলতে পারেন ?
Engreji bolte paren ?

I don't understand Bengali.
আমি বাংলা বুঝি না।
Ami Bangla bujhi na.

Could you please speak more slowly ?
আরো একটু ধীরে বোলবেন?
Aro ektu dhirey bolben ?

I can't speak Bengali.
আমি বাংলা বোলতে পারি না।
Ami Bangla bolte pari na.

Are you married ?
আপনি কি বিবাহিত ?
Apni ki bibahito ?

What is your age ?
আপনার বয়স কত ?
Apnar boyos kato ?

I am 25 years old.
আমার বয়স পঁচিশ বছর।
Amar boyos pachis bochhor.

Have you come for the first time here ?
এখানে কি এই প্রথম এসেছেন।
Ekhane ki ei prothom esechhen ?

How long do you plan to stay ?
কতদিন থাকার পরিকল্পনা আছে?
Kato din thakar parikalpana achhe ?

Where you waiting for me ?
আপনারা কি আমার জন্য অপেক্ষা করছিলেন?
Apnara ki amar jonno apekkha korchhilen ?

Tomorrow is my last day here.
আগামী এখানে আমার শেষ দিন।
Agami al ekhane amar last din.

I am here with my family.
আমি এখানে সপরিবারে আছি।
Ami ekhane saparibar-e achhi.

This is my friend.
ইনি আমার বন্ধু।
Eni amar bandhu.

This is my husband / wife.
ইনি আমার স্বামী / স্ত্রী।
Eni amar Sami / Stri.

Chapter 37

Greetings অভিবাদন (abhibadon)

All the best.
অল দা বেস্ট।
All da best.

And the same to you.
আপনাকেও।
Apnakeo.

Congratulations.
অভিনন্দন
Abhinandan.

Best Wishes.
মঙ্গল কামনা করি।
Mangal Kamona kori.

Good morning / afternoon
সুপ্রভাত / শুভ অপরাহ্ন
Su probhat / Shubho aparano.

Good night.
শুভ রাত্রি
Shubho ratri

Good bye.
বিদায়
Bidai

Happy new year.
শুভ নববর্ষ।
Shubho nabo barsho.

Hope you have had a lovely time.
আশা করি আপনার সময় ভালোই কাটছে।
Asa kori apnar samoi bhaloi katchhe.

Have a happy journey
যাত্রা শুভ হোক।
Jatra shubho hok

I am pleased to meet you.
আপনার দেখা পেয়ে খুশী হলাম।
Apnar dekha peye khushi holam

Chapter 38

Cardinal Numbers

সংখ্যা

English	Bengali	Pronunciation
1. one	এক	ek
2. two	দুই	dui
3. three	তিন	tin
4. four	চার	cha'r
5. five	পাঁচ	panch
6. six	ছয়	chhoy
7. seven	সাত	sat
8. eight	আট	aat
9. nine	নয়	noi
10. ten	দশ	dash
11. eleven	এগারো	egaro

12.	twelve	বারো	bar-o
13.	thirteen	তেরো	tero
14.	fourteen	চৌদ্দ	chouddo
15.	fifteen	পনেরো	panero
16.	sixteen	ষোল	sholo
17.	seventeen	সতেরো	satero
18.	eighteen	আঠারো	atharo
19.	nineteen	উনিশ	unish
20.	twenty	কুড়ি	kuri
21.	twenty-one	একুশ	ekush
22.	twenty two	বাইশ	baish
23.	twenty three	তেইশ	teish
24.	twenty four	চবিবশ	chabbish
25.	twenty five	পঁচিশ	panchish
26.	twenty six	ছাবিবশ	chhabbish
27.	twenty seven	সাতাশ	satash

28.	twenty eight	আঠাশ	athash
29.	twenty nine	ঊনত্রিশ	unatrish
30.	thirty	ত্রিশ	trish
31.	thirty one	একত্রিশ	ekotrish
32.	thirty two	বত্রিশ	botrish
33.	thirty three	তেত্রিশ	tetrish
34.	thirty four	চৌত্রিশ	chautrish
35.	thirty five	পঁয়ত্রিশ	poitrish
36.	thirty six	ছত্রিশ	chhatrish
37.	thirty seven	সাঁইত্রিশ	saitrish
38.	thirty eight	আটত্রিশ	atrish
39.	thirty nine	ঊনচল্লিশ	uno-challish
40.	forty	চল্লিশ	challish
41.	forty one	একচল্লিশ	ek-challish
42.	forty two	বিয়াল্লিশ	biallish
43.	forty three	তেতাল্লিশ	tetallish

44.	forty four	চুয়াল্লিশ	chuallish
45.	forty five	পঁয়তাল্লিশ	poitallish
46.	forty six	ছেচল্লিশ	chhechallish
47.	forty seven	সাতচল্লিশ	satchallish
48.	forty eight	আটচল্লিশ	at-challish
49.	forty nine	ঊনপঞ্চাশ	uno-panchash
50.	fifty	পঞ্চাশ	panchash
51.	fifty one	একান্ন	ekanno
52.	fifty two	বাহান্ন	bahanno
53.	fifty three	তিপান্ন	tippanno
53.	fifty four	চুয়ান্ন	chuanno
55.	fifty five	পঞ্চান্ন	panchanno
56.	fifty six	ছাপান্ন	chhappanno
57.	fifty seven	সাতান্ন	satanno
58.	fifty eight	আটান্ন	atanno
59.	fifty nine	ঊনষাট	uno-shat

60.	sixty	ষাট	shat
61.	sixty one	একষট্টি	ek-shatti
62.	sixty two	বাষট্টি	ba-shatti
63.	sixty three	তেষট্টি	te-shatti
64.	sixty four	চৌষট্টি	chou-satti
65.	sixty five	পঁয়ষট্টি	pai-shatti
66.	sixty six	ছেষট্টি	chhe-shatti
67.	sixty seven	সাতষট্টি	sat-shatti
68.	sixty eight	আটষট্টি	at-shatti
69.	sixty nine	ঊনসত্তর	uno-sattor
70.	seventy	সত্তর	sattor
71.	seventy one	একাত্তর	ek-attor
72.	seventy two	বাহাত্তর	ba-hattor
73.	seventy three	তিয়াত্তর	ti-hattor
74.	seventy four	চুয়াত্তর	chu-hattor
75.	seventy five	পঁচাত্তর	panch-attor

76.	seventy six	ছিয়াত্তর	chhi-attor
77.	seventy seven	সাতাত্তর	sat-attor
78.	seventy eight	আটাত্তর	at-attor
79.	seventy nine	উনআশী	uno-ashi
80.	eighty	আশী	ashi
81.	eighty one	একাশী	ek-ashi
82.	eighty two	বিরাশী	bir-ashi
83.	eighty three	তিরাশী	tir-ashi
84.	eighty four	চুরাশী	chur-ashi
85.	eighty five	পঁচাশী	panch-ashi
86.	eighty six	ছিয়াশী	chhi-ashi
87.	eighty seven	সাতাশী	sat-ashi
88.	eighty eight	আটাশী	at-ashi
89.	eighty nine	উননববই	uno-nobboi
90.	ninety	নববই	nobboi
91.	ninety one	একানববই	eka-nabboi

92.	ninety two	বিরানববই	bira-nabboi
93.	ninety three	তিরানববই	tira-nabboi
94.	ninety four	চুরানববই	chura-nabboi
95.	ninety five	পঁচানববই	pancha-nabboi
96.	ninety six	ছিয়ানববই	chhia-nabboi
97.	ninety seven	সাতানববই	sata-nabboi
98.	ninety eight	আটানববই	ata-nabboi
99.	ninety nine	নিরানববই	nira-nabboi
100.	hundred	একশ	ek-show

500.	Five hundred	পাঁচশ	panchsho
1000.	One thousand	এক হাজার	Ek hazar
100000.	One lac	এক লাখ	Ek lakh

Chapter 39

Ordinal Numbers
পূরণবাচক সংখ্যা (Puronbachak Sankhya)

English	Bengali	Pronunciation
First	প্রথম	Protham
Second	দ্বিতীয়	Ditiya
Third	তৃতীয়	Tritiyo
Fourth	চতুর্থ	Choturtho
Fifth	পঞ্চম	Pancham
Sixth	ষষ্ঠ	Sastha
Seventh	সপ্তম	Saptam
Eighth	অষ্টম	Astam
Nineth	নবম	Nabom
Tehth	দশম	Dasam
Eleventh	একাদশ	Ekadash

Twelfth	দ্বাদশ	Dadash
Thirteenth	ত্রয়োদশ	Trayodosh
Fourteenth	চতুর্দশ	Chaturdash
Fifteenth	পঞ্চদশ	Panchodash
Sixteenth	ষোড়শ	Sodash
Seventeenth	সপ্তদশ	Saptodash
Eighteenth	অষ্টাদশ	Astadash
Nineteenth	ঊনবিংশ	Unobinsho
Twentieth	বিংশ	Binsho
Twenty first	একবিংশ	Ekobinsho
Twenty fifth	পঞ্চবিংশতি	Pancho binsho

Chapter 40

Colours রঙ (Rong)

English	Bengali	Pronunciation
White	সাদা	Sada
Black	কালো	Kalo
Red	লাল	Lal
Blue	নীল	neel
Yellow	হলুদ	Halud
Green	সবুজ	Sabuj
Orange	কমলা	Kamala
Pink	গোলাপী	Golapi
Violet	বেগুনী	Beguni
Brown	বাদামী	Badami
Grey	ধূসর	Dhusar
Ash	ছাই রং	Chhai rong

Crimson	ঘোর লাল	Ghor lal
Scarlet	টকটকে লাল	Tok Toke Lal
Purple	রক্তাভ	Raktabha
Light Red	ফিকে লাল	Fikey lal
Saffron	জাফরানী	Zafrani
Chocolate	খয়েরী	Khayeri
Pale	ফ্যাকাশে	Fakasey
Deep Colour	গাঢ় রং	Garo Rong
Light Colour	হালকা রং	Halka Rong
Mixed Colour	মিশ্রিত রং	Misrito Rong
Golden	সোনালী	Sonali
Sky	আকাশী	Akashi

He has stood first in examination.
সে পরীক্ষায় প্রথম হয়েছে।
Se parikshay protohom hoyechhe.

I read in class ten.
আমি দশম শ্রেণীতে পড়ি।
Ami dashom sreni-te pari

Try again for the second tijme.
দ্বিতীয় বারের জন্য আবার চেষ্টা কর।
Ditiyo bar-er janyo abar chesta karo.

We broaded on a third-clas compartment.
আমরা একটা তৃতীয় শ্রেণীর কামরাতে উঠেছিলাম।
Amra ekta tritiyo shrenir kamrai uthechhilam

Boys started shouting at the top of their voice.
ছেলেরা সপ্তম সুরে চেঁচাতে লাগলো।
Chhelera saptom sur-e checharte laglo.

We have entered in twenty first century.
আমরা একবিংশ শতাব্দীতে প্রবেশ করেছি।
Amra eko binsho shatabdi-te probesh korechhi.

I had a black and white tv
আমার একটা সাদাকালো টিভি ছিল।
Amar ekta sada-kalo tv chhilo.

Jaipur is called the Pink City of India.
জয়পুরকে ভারতের গোলাপী শহর বলা হয়।
Jaipur-ke Bharat-er golapi shahar bola hoi.

I like to wear light-colour dress.
আমি হাল্কা রংয়ের পোশাক পরতে পছন্দ করি।
Ami halka ronger poshak porte pasando kori.

The sky is blue in colour.
আকাশের রঙ নীল।
Akash-er rong neel.

You look beautiful in yellow dress.
হলুদ পোশাকে তোমাকে সুন্দর দেখায়।
Halud poshak-e tomake sundor dekhai.

He wore a brown cap.
সে একটা বাদামী টুপি পরেছিল।
Se ekta badami tupi porechilo.

We saw black clouds in the sky.
আমরা আকাশে কালো মেঘ দেখলাম।
Amra akash-e kalo megh dekhlam.

This is a white shirt
এটা একটা সাদা জামা
Eta ekta sada jama

My sweater is of green colour
আমার সোয়েটারটি নীল রঙের
Amar sweater-ti nil ronger

Chapter 41

Spices
রঙ (Masela)

English	Bengali	Pronunciation
Chilli	লঙ্কা	Lanka
Black-Pepper	গোল মরিচ	Gol marich
Red-Pepper	শুকনো লঙ্কা	Sukno Lanka
Turmeric	হলুদ	Halud
Cardamon	এলাচ	Elachi
Clove	লবঙ্গ	Labango
Coriander Seed	ধনে	Dhone
Cumin Seed	জিরা	Zira
Cassia leaf	তেজপাতা	Tej pata
Aniseed	মৌরী	Mauri
Mustard	সরষে	Sarse
Parsely	রাঁধুনী	Radhuni

Cinnamon	দারুচিনি	Daruchini
Salt	লবণ	Laban
Rock Salt	সৈন্দব লবণ	Saindhav Laban
Saffron	জাফরান	Jafran
Mace	জৈত্রী	Jaitri
Nutmeg	জায়ফল	Jaifal
Musk	কস্তুরী	Kasturi
Cubeb	কাবাব চিনি	Kabab Chini
Ginger	আদা	Ada
Garlic	রসুন	Rasun
Fenugreek	মেথী	Methi
Long Pepper	পিপুল	Pipul
Camphor	কর্পূর	Karpur
Betel leaf	পান	Paan
Betel nut	সুপারী	Supari
Catechu	খয়ের	Khaer
Tamarind	তেঁতুল	Tatul

I want to purchase some spices

আমি কিছু মশলা কিনতে চাই।

Ami kichhu masla kinte chai.

Please add some more salt in soup.

ঝোলে আর একটু লবণ দাও।

Jhol-e ar ektu laban dao.

Bring ginger and garlic today.

আজ আদা ও রসুন এনো।

Aj ada o rosun eno.

India is a country of spices.

ইণ্ডিয়া মশলার দেশ।

India maslar desh.

This curry is enriched with spices.

তরকারীটাতে মশলা বেশী পড়েছে।

Torkary ta-te masla besi parechhe.

I can't do without spices.

মশলা ছাড়া আমার চলে না।

Masla chharo amar chale na.

Indians use spices in water also.
ইণ্ডিয়ানরা জলেও মশলা দিয়ে পান করে।
Indian ra jal-eo masla diye paan kore.

Too much spices spoil the dish
বেশী মশলায় খাবারের স্বাদ নষ্ট হয়।
Besi moslai khabar-er swad nosto hoi

Spicy foods are bedoming popular
মশলাদার খাবার জনপ্রিয় হচ্ছে।
Mosladar khabar janpriyo hochchhe

Bengalees fond of poppy seeds.
বাঙালীরা পোস্তো খেতে ভালবাসে
Bangali-ra posto kheta bhalobase.

Chapter 42

Transport and Communication

রঙ (Paribahan o Jogajog)

English	Bengali	Pronunciation
Aeroplane	উড়োজাহাজ	Urojahaj
Boat	নৌকা	Nauka
Car	গাড়ি	Gari
Bus	বাস	Bus
Cycle	সাইকেল	Cycle
Helicopter	হেলিকপ্টার	Helicopter
Horse Cart	টাঙ্গা	Tonga
Ship	জাহাজ	Jahaj
Parachute	প্যারাস্যুট	Parasut
Train	ট্রেন	Train

Tram	ট্রাম	Trum
Rickshaw	রিক্সা	Riksa
Jeep	জিপ	Jeep
Motor cycle	মোটর সাইকেল	Motor cycle

I came by aeroplane.
আমি উড়োজাহাজে এসেছি।
Ami Uro-jahaj-e esechhi.

I like riding bicycle.
আমি সাইকেল চড়তে ভালোবাসি।
Ami cycle chorte bhalobasi.

We will go by horse cart.
আমরা ঘোড়ার গাড়িতে যাবো।
Amra ghorar garite jabo.

Rickshaws are common in town
শহরে প্রচুর রিকসা
Shahar-e prochur rickshaw

Chapter 43

About Education
শিক্ষা সম্বন্ধীয় (Shiksha Sambandhiya)

English	Bengali	Pronunciation
Education	শিক্ষা	Shiksha
Teacher	শিক্ষক	Shikshak
School	বিদ্যালয়	Vidyalaya
College	মহাবিদ্যালয়	Mahavidyalaya
University	বিশ্ববিদ্যালয়	Vishwavidyalaya
Professor	অধ্যাপক	Adhyapak
Principal	অধ্যক্ষ	Adhyaksha
Mistress	শিক্ষিকা	Shikshika
Student	ছাত্র/ছাত্রী	Chhatra /Chhatri
Sum	অঙ্ক	Anka
Drawing	অঙ্কন	Ankan
Present	উপস্থিত	Upasthit

Absent	অনুপস্থিত	Anupasthit
Text-book	পাঠ্যপুস্তক	Pathya-pustak
Admission	ভর্তি	Bhorti
Prize	পুরস্কার	Puraskár
Punishment	শাস্তি	Shasti
Ink	কালি	Kali
Dictionary	অভিধান	Abhidhan
Paper	কাগজ	Kagaz
Chalk	খড়িমাটি	Khari Mati
Medal	পদক	Padak
Question	প্রশ্ন	Prasna
Answer	উত্তর	Uttar
Page	বইয়ের পাতা	Boier Pata
Book	বই	Boi
Stanza	স্তবক	Stabak
Line	ছত্র	Chhotra

Are you going to school ?
তুমি কি স্কুলে যাচ্ছো ?
Tumi ki School-e jachcho ?

I want to buy an Englisht to Bengali dictionary
আমি একখানা ইংরাজীবাংলা অভিধান কিনতে চাই।
Ami ek-khana Engraji-Bangla abhidhan kinte chai.

My friend is a student of this school.
আমার বন্ধু এই স্কুলের ছাত্র।
Amar Bandhu ei school-er chhatro.

Have you heard the name of Nalanda University ?
আপনি কি নালন্দা বিশ্ববিদ্যালয়ের নাম শুনেছেন ?
Apni ki Nalanda Viswavidyalaya-er nam sunechhen ?

I want to get some white paper.
আমি কয়েকটা সাদা কাগজ চাই।
Ami kayekta sada kagaz chai.

Mr. Roy is a professor of English
মিঃ রায় ইংরেজীর একজন অধ্যাপক
Mr. Roy engrejir ekjon adhyapak.

He is an expert in Drawing
তিনি অঙ্কন বিদ্যায় পারদর্শী
Tini ankan vidya-y parodorshi.

I reside beside a college
আমি একটা কলেজের কাছে থাকি
Ami Ekta college-er kachhe thaki

I am a teacher of a school
আমি স্কুলের একজন শিক্ষক
Ami school-er ekjon sikkhok

Our's is a co-ed. School.
আমাদের স্কুলে ছেলে মেয়েরা একসাথে পড়ে
Amader school-e chale mayera eaksathe pore.

Chapter 44

Profession

পেশা (Pesha)

English	Bengali	Pronunciation
Farmer	কৃষক	Krishak
Fisherman	জেলে	Jele
Labourer	মজুর	Majur
Milkman	গোয়ালা	Goala
Oilman	কলু	Kalhu
Potter	কুমোর	Kumar
Blacksmith	কামার	Kamar
Carpenter	সূত্রধর	Sutradhar
Goldsmith	স্বর্ণকার	Sarnakar
Weaver	তাঁতী	Tanti
Barber	নাপিত	Napit

Gardener	মালী	Mali
Tailor	দরজী	Dorji
Sweeper	ঝাড়ুদার	Jharudar
Cook	পাচক	Pachak
Porter	মুটে	Mutey
Priest	পুরোহিত	Purohit
Nurse	সেবিকা	Sebika
Washerman	ধোপা	Dhopa
Cobbler	মুচি	Muchi
Gate-keeper	দারোয়ান	Darwan
Clerk	কেরাণী	Kerani
Printer	মুদ্রক	Mudrak
Painter	চিত্রকর	Chitrakar
Shop Keeper	দোকানদার	Dokandar
Singer	গায়ক	Gayak
Artist	শিল্পী	Shilpi

Actor	অভিনেতা	Abhineta
Dancer	নর্তকী	Nartaki
Butcher	কসাই	Kasai
Thatcher	ঘরামী	Gharami
Broker	দালাল	Dalal
Jeweller	জহুরী	Jahuri
Book-binder	দপ্তরী	Daptari
Hawker	ফেরীওয়ালা	Feriwala
Hunter	শিকারী	Shikari
Grocer	মুদি	Mudi
Mason	রাজমিস্ত্রী	Rajmistri
Baker	রুটিওয়ালা	Ruti-wala
Confectioner	ময়রা	Moira
Magician	যাদুকর	Jadukar
Stationer	মনোহার	Manohar
Fortune teller	গণক	Ganak

Money lender	মহাজন	Mahajan
Perfumer	গন্ধ বণিক	Gandha banik
Director	পরিচালক	Parichalak
Producer	প্রযোজক	Prajojak
Orator	বক্তা	Bakta
Player	খেলোয়াড়	Kheloar
Dramatist	নাট্যকার	Natyakar
Novelist	ঔপন্যাসিক	Oupannasik
Palmist	হস্তরেখাবিদ্	Hastarekha-bid
Driver	চালক	Chalok

Hawkers have occupied foot-path
হকারেরা ফুটপাথ কব্জা করেছে
Hawker-era footpath kobja korechhe

P. C. Sorkar was a machician
পি. সি. সরকার ছিলেন জাদুকর
P. C. Sorkar chhilen jadukor

Chapter 45

Things to remember
মনে রাখার বিষয় (Mone rakhar bisoy)

How are you ?.
কেমন আছেন ?
Kemon aachhen ?

Where are you going ?
কোথায় যাচ্ছেন ?
Kothai jachhen ?

Where is the market ?
বাজার কোনদিকে ?
Bazar kon dikey ?

Are you coming from Europe ?
আপনি ক ইউরোপ থেকে আসছেন ?
Apni ki Europe theke aschhen ?

When have you come here ?
আপনি এখানে কবে এসেছেন ?
Ekhane apni kobe esechhen ?

May I help you ?
আপনাকে সাহায্য করবো কি ?
Apnake sahajjo korbo ki ?

Please help me.
দয়া করে আমাকে সাহায্য করুন।
Daya kore amake sahajjo korun.

I am sorry !
আমি দুঃখিত !
Ami dukkhito.

Where is the garments shop ?
কাপড়ের দোকান কোনখানে ?
Kapar-er dokan konkhane ?

Show me a coat.
আমাকে একটা কোট দেখান।
Amake ekta kot dekhan.

I like red coat.
আমি লাল কোট পছন্দ করি।
Ami Lal kot pachando kori.

Are you well now ?
ভালো আছেন ?
Bhalo achhen ?

I am quite well.
আমি বেশ ভালোই আছি।
Ami besh bhaloi achhi.

What is your name ?
আপনার নাম কি ?
Apnar naam ki ?

My nake is Gopal.
আমার নাম গোপাল।
Amar naam Gopal.

What do you do ?
আপনি কি করেন ?
Apni ki koren ?

I am a Teacher.
আমি একজন শিক্ষক।
Ami ekjon shikkhok.

Who is he ?
উনি কে ?
Uni ke ?

He is my father.
উনি আমার বাবা।
Eni amar baba.

She is my mother.
উনি আমার মা।
Uni amar maa.

My father is a farmer.
আমার বাবা একজন কৃষক।
Amar baba ekjon krishak.

My mother is a nurse.
আমার মা একজন নার্স।
Amar maa ekjon nurse.

When have you come here ?
আপনি এখানে কবে এসেছেন ?
Apni ekhane kabe esechhen ?

I have come here yesterday.
আমি গতকাল এখানে এসেছি।
Ami goto kal ekhane esechhi.

Which places do yo want to visit ?
কোন কোন জায়গায় আপনি ঘুরতে চান ?
Kon kon jaigai apni ghurte chan ?

How far the Sundarban from Kolkata ?
কোলকাতা থেকে সুন্দরবন কত দূরে ?
Sundarban Kolkata theke koto durey ?

I want to visit Sundarban.
আমি সুন্দরবনে যেতে চাই।
Ami Sundarban-e jete chai.

Do you accompany me ?
আপনি আমার সাথে যাবেন ?
Apni amar sathe jaben ?

Sorry ! I have no time in hand.
দুঃখিত ! আমার হাতে সময় নেই।
Dukkhito ! Amar hate-e samoy nei.

I need your cooperation.
আমি আপনার সহযোগিতা চাই।
Ami apnar Sahajogita chai.

It would be better if you go with me.
আপনি সাথে গেলে বড় ভালো হতো।
Apni sath-e gele boro bhalo hoto.

Is there any hotel near Sundarban ?
সুন্দরবনের কাছে কোন হোটেল আছে ?
Sundarban-er kachhe kono hotel achhe ?

There are guest houses at Pakhirala.
পাখিবালাতে অতিথি নিবাস রয়েছে।
Pakhirala-te atithi niwas royechhe.

How can we go there ?
সেখানে কীভাবে যেতে পারি ?
Sekhane ki-bhabe jete pari ?

We have to go via Gosaba.
গোসাবা হয়ে যেতে হবে।
Gosaba hoye jete hobe.

Rabindranath Tagore was born at the time of Bengal Renasa.
বাংলার রেনেসা'র সময় রবীন্দ্রনাথ জন্মেছিলেন
Banglar renasa-r samoy Rabindranath jonmechilen.

Gold sale is less due to heavy price.
সোনার দাম অত্যন্ত বেশীর জন্য বিক্রী কম।
Sonar dam Atonto basir jonne bikri kom.

What Bengal thinks today, India will thinks tomorrow and the whole world other days.
বাংলা যা আজ ভাববে, ভারত তা আগামীকাল ভাববে এবং সমস্ত বিশ্ব পরে তা ভাববে।
Bangla ja aaj bhabbe, bharat ta agamikal bhabbe abong somosto bishwa pore ta bhabbe.

Rainbow looks beautiful in the sky.
ইন্দ্রধনু (রামধনু) আকাশে দেখতে ভাল লাগে।
Indrodhonush (Ramdhonu) akashe dekhte bhalo lage.

Chapter 46

Filling Form
ফর্ম ভরতি (Form bhorti)

Word	Bengali Meaning	Pronunciation
Name	নাম	Naam
Sarname	পদবী	Padabi
Father's name	বাবার নাম	babar naam
Mother's name	মায়ের নাম	Maa-er naam
Date of birth	জন্ম তারিখ	Janmo tarikh
Place of birth	জন্ম স্থান	Janmo sthan
Address	ঠিকানা	Thikana
Residence	আবাস	abas
Working place	কর্মস্থল	Karmo-sthol
Educational -	শিক্ষাগত-	Shikkhogato-
qualification	যোগ্যতা	joggata

Profession	পেশা	Pesha
Working experience	কাজের অভিজ্ঞতা	Kajer abhigyata
Mother's tongue	মাতৃভাষা	matri-bhasa
Nationality	রাষ্ট্রীয়তা	rastriyata
Religion	ধর্ম	dharmo
Blood Group	রক্তের গ্রুপ	rakter group
Telephone No.	দূরভাষ	Durbhas
Signature	স্বাক্ষর	Sakkhar
Date	তারিখ	tarikh

Chapter 47

Bengal's Sweets
ফর্ম ভরতি (Banglar Misti)

Bengali Name	Pronunciation
সন্দেশ	Sandesh
রসগোল্লা	Raso-golla
রসমালাই	Ros-malai
রসকদম্ব	Ros-kadombo
রসবড়া	Ros-bora
রাজভোগ	Raj-bhog
মোহনভোগ	Mohan-bhog
কমলাভোগ	Kamla-bhog
সীতাভোগ	Sita-bhog
ক্ষীরমোহন	Khir-mohan
সরভাজা	Sar-bhaja

সরপুরিয়া	Sar-puriya
ল্যাংচা	Langcha
ল্যাডিক্যানি	Lady-cani
দরবেশ	Darbesh
দানাদার	Danadar
গুজিয়া	Gujiya
লাড্ডু	Laddu
ছানার পায়েস	Chhanar-payesh
ছানার মুড়কী	Chhanar Murki
ছানার গজা	Chhanar Gaja
মিষ্টি দৈ	Misti Doi
পান্তুয়া	Pantua
চম্‌চম্‌	Chamcham
কাঁচাগোল্লা	Kacha-golla
লবঙ্গ লতিকা	Labango Lotika
জিলিপি	Jilipi

অমৃতি	Amriti
বোঁদে	Bonde
প্যাঁড়া	Pyara
বালুসাই	Balu-sai
মালপোয়া	Malpoa
গুজিয়া	Gujia
রাবড়ি	Rabri
জলভরা তালশাঁস	Jol Bhora Talsash
বরফী	Burfi
মিহিদানা	Mihidana
সীতাভোগ	Sitabhog
চিনি	Chini (Sugar)
বাতাসা	Batasa
নকুলদানা	Nakul-dana
মিছরী	Michhri
পাটালী গুড়	Patali Gur

Chapter 48

Geographic
ফর্ম ভরতি (Bhougolik)

English	Bengali	Pronunciation
Mountain	পর্বত	Parbat
Mountain-range	পর্বতমালা	Parbat-mala
Peak	চূড়া	Chura
Pass	গিরিপথ	Giripath
Glacier	হিমবাহ	Himbaho
Snow-fall	তুষার পাত	Tusharpat
Water-fall	জলপ্রপাত	Jal-propat
Fountain	ঝরণা	Jharna
Spring	প্রস্রবণ	Prasraban
Valley	উপত্যকা	Upatyaka
River	নদী	Nodi

Riverbank	নদীতীর	Noditir
Riverbed	নদীরচর	Nodir-char
Tributory	উপনদী	Upa-nodi
Distributory	শাখানদী	Sakha-nodi
Desert	মরুভূমি	Moru-bhumi
Sand	বালি	Bali
Sand-dune	বালিয়াড়ি	Baliari
Sand-storm	আঁধি	Andhi
Plateau	মালভূমি	Mal-bhumi
Hill	পাহাড়	Pahar
Hillock	টিলা	Tila
Stone	পাথর	Pathor
Pebbles	নুড়ি	Nuri
Plain	সমতল	Samotal
Lake	হ্রদ	Hrod

Marsh	জলাভূমি	Jala-bhumi
Coast	উপকূল	Upakul
Wave	ঢেউ	Dheu
Tide	জোয়ার	Joar
Strait	প্রণালী	Pronali
Isthmas	প্রণালী	Jojak
Canal	নালা	Nala

Chapter 49

Geographic
মহাসাগর, সাগর (Bhougolik)

English	Bengali	Pronunciation
Ocean	মহাসাগর	Mahasagar
Pacific Ocean	প্রশান্ত মহাসাগর	Prosanto Mahasagar
Atlantic Ocean	অতলান্তিক মহাসাগর	Atalantic Mahasagar
Indian Ocean	ভারত মহাসাগর	Bharat Mahasagar
Bay of Bengal	বঙ্গোপসাগর	Bangopa Sagar
Arabian Sea	আরব সাগর	Arab Sagar
Red Sea	লোহিত সাগর	Lohit Sagar
Dead Sea	মরু সাগর	Moru Sagar
Mediternian Sea	ভূমধ্য সাগর	Bhumoddho Sagar

Black Sea	কৃষ্ণ সাগর	Krishno Sagar
Caspian Sea	কাশ্যপ সাগর	Kashyap Sagar
Marmare Sea	মর্মর সাগর	Mormor Sagar
Persian Gulf	পারস্যপোসাগর	Parasya Upasagar
Caspian Sea	কাশ্যপ সাগর	Kashyap Sagar
Marmare Sea	মর্মর সাগর	Mormor Sagar
Persian Gulf	পারস্যপোসাগর	Parasya Upasagar

Chapter 50

Important Towns
গুরুত্বপূর্ণ শহর (Guruttopurno Sahar)

English	Bengali	Pronunciation
Calcutta	কোলকাতা	Kolkata
Bombay	মুম্বাই	Mumbai
Madras	চেন্নাই	Chennai
Hardwar	হরিদ্বার	Haridwar
Lucknow	লক্ষ্ণৌ (লখ্নৌ)	Lokhnau
Mymensigh	ময়মনসিংহ	Moymonsingha
Chittagong	চট্টগ্রাম	Chatto gram
Burdwan	বর্ধমান	Bordhoman
English Bazar	ইংরেজ বাজার	Engrej Bazar
Kontai	কাঁথি	Kanthi
Mysore	মহীশূর	Mohisur
Awadh	অযোধ্যা	Ajoddha
Cape Camorin	কন্যা কুমারী	Konya Kumari
Jessore	যশোর	Jasore

Chapter 51

A few English Proverbs with their Bengali Equivalents

1. A bad workman quarrels with his tools.
2. A burnt child dreads the fire.
3. A drop in the ocean.
4. A figure among cyphers.
5. A frog can not be dispelled by a fan.
6. A honey tongue, a heart of gall
7. A little knowledge is a dangerous thing.
8. All's well that ends well.
9. An empty vessel sounds much.
10. As the king so are the subjects.
11. As you sow, so you reap.

12. Barking dogs seldom bite.

13. Beggars could not be choosers.

14. Birds of a feather flock together.

15. Black will take no other hue.

16. Contentment is happiness.

17. Crows are never the whiter for washing.

18 Cut your coat according to your cloth.

19. Do evil and look for it.

20. Forced labour is better than idleness.

21. Fortune favours the brave.

22. Half a loaf is better than no bread.

23. Ill got, ill spent.

24. It is hard to live in Rome and to fight with the Pope.

25. It makes two to make a quarrel.

26. Killing two birds with one stone.

27. Like curves like.

28. Like father, like son.

29. Living from hand to mouth.

30. Many men, many mind.

31. Might is right.

32. Misfortunes never come alone.

33. Money begets money.

34. No pains, no gains.

35. One flower makes no garland.

36. One nail drives out another.

37. Poverty breeds strife.

38. Riches have wings.

39. Steal a goose and give giblets in alms.

40. Strike the iron while it is hot.

41. The innocent have nothing to fear.

42. To make a mountain of a mole-hill.

43. Too make cooks spoils the broth.

44. To rob Peter to pay Paul.

45. Union is strength.

Bengali Equivalents

১. নাচতে না জানলে উঠোন বাঁকা।

২. ঘরপোড়া গরু সিঁদুরে মেঘ দেখলে ডরায়।

৩. সিন্ধুতে বিন্দু।

৪. অন্ধদের মধ্যে কানা রাজা।

৫. ব্যাঙকে দেখিও না ঠাণ্ডার ভয়

৬. মুখে মধু, অন্তরে বিষ।

৭. অল্প বিদ্যা ভয়ংকরী।

৮. যার শেষ ভালো তার সব ভালো।

৯. খালি কলসী বাজে বেশী।

১০. যেমন রাজা তেমন প্রজা।

১১. যেমন কর্ম, তেমন ফল।

১২. যত গর্জায়, তত বর্ষায় না।

১৩. ভিক্ষার চাল কাঁড়া না আকাঁড়া।

১৪. চোরে চোরে মাসতুতো ভাই।

১৫. কালো কখনও রং বদলায় না।

১৬. সন্তোষেই পরম সুখ।

১৭. কয়লা ধুলেও ময়লা যায় না।

১৮. আয় বুঝে ব্যায় কর।

১৯. পাপ করলে ফল পাবে।

২০. বেকার থাকার চেয়ে বেগার দেওয়া ভালো।

২১. বীরভোগ্যা বসুন্ধরা।

২২. নেই মামার চেয়ে কানা মামা ভালো

২৩. পাপের ধন, প্রায়শ্চিত্তে যায়।

২৪. জলে বাস করে কুমিরের সাথে ঝগড়া

২৫. এক হাতে তালি বাজে না।

২৬. এক ঢিলে দুই পাখি মারা।

২৭. বিষে বিষে বিষক্ষয়।

২৮. যেমন বাপ, তেমন বেটা।

২৯. নুন আনতে পান্তা ফুরোয়।

৩০. নানা মুনির নানা মত।

৩১. জোর যার মুল্লুক তার।

৩২. বিপদ কখনো একা আসে না

৩৩. টাকায় টাকা হয়। জলে জল বাঁধে।

৩৪. দুঃখ বিনা সুখ লাভ হয় না।

৩৫. এক ফুলে মালা গাঁথা যায় না

৩৬. কাঁটা দিয়ে কাঁটা তোলা যায়

৩৭. অভাবে স্বভাব নষ্ট।

৩৮. লক্ষ্মী চঞ্চলা।

৩৯. জরু মেরে গরু দান।

৪০. রোদ থাকতে খড় শুকিয়ে নাও

৪১. ল্যাংটার নেই বাটপাড়ের ভয়

৪২. তিলকে তাল করা।

৪৩. অধিক সন্ন্যাসীতে গাজন নষ্ট

৪৪. গরু মেরে জুতো দান।

৪৫. একতাই বল।

Bengali Equivalents

1. Nach-te na janle uthon banka
2. Ghar pora goru sindure megh dekhle doray.
3. Sindu-te bindu.
4. Andhoder moddhe kana raja.
5. Bang-ke dekhio-na thandar bhoy
6. Mukh-e modhu antare bish.
7. Alpo bidya vayankari.
8. Jar shesh bhalo tar sob bhalo.
9. Khali Kolsi baje beshi.
10. Jamon raja, temon proja.
11. Jamon karmo, temon fal.
12. Jato garjay tato borshai na.
13. Vikhkhar chal kara na akara.
14. Chore chore mastuto bhai.

15. Kalo kakhano rong badlay na

16. Santosh-ei param sukh.

17. Koyla dhule-o moyla jai na.

18. Aye bhuje byay karo.

19. Pap korle fall pabey.

20. Bekar thakar cheya begar dewa bhalo.

21. Bir bhogya basundhara.

22. Nei mamar cheye kana mama bhalo.

23. Paper dhan prayeschitte jai.

24. Jal-e bas kore kumir-er sathe jhagra.

25. Ek hat-e tali baje na.

26. Ek dhil-e dui pakhi mara.

27. Bis-e bis-e bisakkhoy.

28. Jemon bap, tamon beta.

29. Nun ante panta phuroe.

30. Nana munir nana mot.

31. Jor jar mulluk tar.

32. Bipod kakhono eka ase na

33. Takae taka hoi. Jole jal bandhe.

34. Dukkho bina sukh labh hoi na.

35. Ek phule mala gatha jai na.

36. Kanta diye kanta tola jai.

37. Abhab e sabhab nasto.

38. Lakkhi chanchala.

39. Joru mere goru daan.

40. Rode thakte khar sukhiye nao.

41. Langtar nei batparer bhoi.

42. Til-ke tal kora.

43. Odhik sanyasi te gajon nasto.

44. Goru mere juto daan.

45. Ekatai bol.

Chapter 52

Model Letter
Personal correspondence

A letter to a guide who helped me to visit Delhi.

New Delhi
15th March 2013

Dear Kanjilal,

Many thanks to you for your kind co-operation during my Delhi tour. It is you who has helped me to know a lot about the glorious past of this old city. Your deep knowledge about those monuments benefited me in many ways.

Thank you once again for your kind co-operation and a good companionship. Hope we meet again.

Yours sincerely
Johnson

ব্যক্তিগত পত্র

দিল্লী দর্শনে সাহায্যকারী গাইডকে পত্র।

নিউ দিল্লী
১৫ই মার্চ ২০১৩

প্রিয় কাঞ্জিলাল,

দিল্লীতে ভ্রমণকালে আপনার সহযোগিতার কথা মনে করে আপনাকে ধন্যবাদ জানাচ্ছি। আপনি আমাকে দিল্লীর গৌরবময় অতীত সম্বন্ধে জানতে সাহায্য করেছেন। আপনার গভীর জ্ঞান আমাকে অনেক দিক থেকে সাহায্য করেছে।

সহযোগিতার জন্য আর একবার আপনাকে ধন্যবাদ জানাই। আশা করি পরে আবার দেখা হবে।

ইতি
আপনার প্রিয়
জনসন

Byaktigato Patra

Delhi darshan-e sahajyo kari guide ke patro.

New Delhi
15th March 2013

Priyo Kanjilal,

Dilli-te bhromon kale apnar sahajogitar katha mone kore apnake dhonnobad janachchhi. Apni amake dilli-r gaurav moy atit samarke jante sahajjo koechhen. Apnar govir gyan amake anek dik theke sahajjo korechhe.

Sahajogitar janno ar ekbar apnake dhannobad janai. Asha kori pore abar dekha hobe.

eti
Apnar Priyo-

সমাপ্ত